LAURA CANDLER'S
GRAPHIC ORGANIZERS FOR READING

LAURA CANDLER'S
GRAPHIC ORGANIZERS FOR READING

TEACHING TOOLS ALIGNED
WITH THE COMMON CORE

COMPASS

A DIVISION OF BRIGANTINE MEDIA

Published by Compass, an imprint of Brigantine Media
211 North Avenue, Saint Johnsbury, Vermont 05819

Cover and book design by Jacob L. Grant

Printed in Canada

For more information about site licenses or multiple copies,
visit the resource page online for this book:
www.lauracandler.com/gofr
or
Brigantine Media
211 North Avenue
Saint Johnsbury, Vermont 05819
Phone: 802-751-8802
E-mail: neil@brigantinemedia.com
Website: www.brigantinemedia.com

Acknowledgments

Graphic Organizers for Reading is so much more than a book of printables, and I want to offer my sincere gratitude to those who contributed to its creation. This book was originally intended to be a chapter in *Laura Candler's Power Reading Workshop: A Step-by-Step Guide*, but it quickly became apparent that graphic organizers were worthy of their own book. After *Power Reading Workshop* was published, I began working on this manuscript, and I once again turned to the Empowering Readers Learning Community for help and feedback. *Graphic Organizers for Reading* bears the "Field Tested - Teacher Approved" stamp for a reason; everything in it has been tested in the classroom and tweaked to perfection by me or members of this discussion group. I am indebted to so many of those teachers, including those named below, who contributed to this book's final form. Whether they tested the graphic organizers with their students, suggested instructional strategies, or proofread the final version, the individuals below helped shape this book into a wonderful and very practical tool for teachers. I want to express special thanks to my friend and workshop director Pat Calfee for her guidance in the area of lesson design and the creation of effective mini-lessons. Thanks to my former students Halle Auf Der Heide and Taylor Williams, whose original work is used to create the illustrations on pages 66, 70, and 131. Finally, I want to thank Janis Raye, Neil Raphel, and Jacob Grant of Brigantine Media for transforming my original self-published e-book into a professionally-designed and printed literary work of art! Writing this book has definitely been a collaborative process, and I've enjoyed sharing my journey with an amazing group of people!

Laura Candler

Pat Calfee
Washington, NC

Ann Goldbach
Liberty Township, OH

Kerry Brown
Norwalk, CT

Sue Roberts
Chicago, IL

Francie Kugelman
Los Angeles, CA

Jewelia Oswald
Topeka, KS

Jo-Ann Mumford
Truro, Nova Scotia

Jeanellen Henry
Falling Waters, WV

Judith Rowe
Perth, Australia

Linda Bruno
Bristol, RI

Saundra McDonald
Salt Lake City, UT

Sheri Seyler
Glendora, CA

Kristin Sheets
Angola, IN

Kristi Swartz
Loveland, OH

Lisa McKenna
Park Ridge, NJ

Carmen Doerr
Katy, TX

Jenny Owens
Cumming, GA

Nancy Dravenstott
Smithville, OH

Joan Krogman
Ogden, UT

Sharon Porter
Rutherfordton, NC

Shellie Sallas
Phoenix, AZ

Ashley Fulp
Hutto, TX

Kay Sims
Kennesaw, GA

Jennifer Laurence
Phoenix, AZ

Mary Welken
Bluffton, SC

Jana Wilson
Marion, AR

Carolyn Wilhelm
Maple Grove, MN

Shari Couturier
Fayetteville, NC

Kim Lesser
Brooklyn, NY

Stacey Sawyer
Clayton, NC

Susan Rosenthal
Miami, FL

Sandy Brown
Fountain Hills, AZ

Diane Evers
Palmyra, NJ

Lisa Waddill
Austin, TX

INTRODUCTION

• • • • • • • • •

Graphic organizers come in all shapes and sizes, from poster-sized charts to folded pieces of paper that tuck into your pocket. But whatever they look like, all graphic organizers serve the same general purpose: to help organize and conceptualize information. They are tools to help connect new ideas to previously-learned concepts, which results in higher retention of information and leads to new insights.

In my experience as a classroom teacher, I have found graphic organizers to be extremely powerful tools in all subject areas. They are particularly effective for teaching reading strategies and for applying those skills in content areas like science, health, and social studies. Students enjoy creating and completing graphic organizers, and often refer to them during class discussions or when talking about their work with a partner or team. Graphic organizers introduce an element of excitement and fun into any lesson!

Graphic organizers can be included in almost any reading program: the Reading Workshop approach, Literature Circles, small groups and centers, or teaching from a basal reader. They are especially useful for visual learners who need to see new information organized and mapped out in ways that make sense to them.

Graphic organizers can be used to teach almost any reading strategy or skill. Some graphic organizers, like the Character Trait Map, have a specific purpose and are used in a certain way. Others, like the Venn diagram, are more generic and can be adapted for a number of uses.

In *Graphic Organizers for Reading: Teaching Tools Aligned with the Common Core*, you'll find effective strategies for using graphic organizers to meet the Common Core Standards for grades 2 through 6. Almost every state has adopted the Common Core Standards. Every one of the Common Core Standards for Informational Text and Literature can be taught using one or more of the graphic organizers in this book.

One of the best things about using graphic organizers is that they make lesson planning a breeze! Take a look at what you'll learn:

Chapter 1 – Teaching with Graphic Organizers – This chapter shows you easy strategies for creating Common Core mini-lessons from nothing more than a graphic organizer and a short reading selection. I'll walk you through this with an example using a well-known children's book about the rain forest, *Nature's Green Umbrella*. At the end of Chapter 1 are grade-level charts that show the Common Core Reading Standards for Informational Text and Literature, and the graphic organizers that can be used to help teach each Standard. Every Common Core Reading Standard has at least one graphic organizer you can use, and many have several you can choose.

Chapter 2 – Multi-purpose Graphic Organizers – Seven different multi-purpose graphic organizers are included in this chapter, along with ways to use them specifically for reading instruction. In Chapter 2, you'll also learn how to teach your students to select the best graphic organizer for a particular text.

Chapter 3 – Graphic Organizers for Informational Text and Literature – This chapter has a wealth of specific graphic organizers for teaching informational texts and literature. You can select the graphic organizer that will serve as the best tool for teaching a particular Common Core Reading Standard, or for teaching many reading strategies. The Informational Text graphic organizers can also be used with almost any content text, such as science, social studies, or health.

Supplementary Online Resources – Visit **www.lauracandler.com/gofr** to find online resources to supplement the text: downloadable copies of the Common Core Standards/Graphic Organizers charts, printer-friendly versions of some of the graphic organizers, and information about obtaining a site license for this book for your school or district. All downloadable pages are noted in this book at the bottom of the page with this icon:

This book will give you one or more graphic organizers to help teach every Common Core Standard for Reading. It will also guide you through all the steps for using each of the organizers, so you can integrate them into your lesson planning. In no time at all, you and your students will be tapping into the power of graphic organizers!

CHAPTER 1

Teaching with Graphic Organizers

Teaching with Graphic Organizers

• • • • • • • • •

Graphic organizers are powerful instructional aids that add an extra dimension to your reading program. But they need to be introduced properly to your students to be fully effective. Although graphic organizers may seem intuitive to adults, students need specific instruction in how to use them. Once they are familiar with a graphic organizer, you can utilize it as part of your reading lessons.

Graphic Organizers as Teaching Tools for the Common Core Standards

The Common Core State Standards have been widely adopted in the U.S. As of early 2012, 45 states, the District of Columbia, and the U.S. Virgin Islands have adopted the Standards. The Common Core Standards outline *what* to teach, but they don't specify *how* to meet those objectives. As stated on the Common Core State Standards Initiative website, "By emphasizing required achievements, the Standards leave room . . . to determine how those goals should be reached. . . . Teachers are thus free to provide students with whatever tools and knowledge their professional judgment and experience identify as most helpful for meeting the goals set out in the Standards."

The developers of the Common Core are to be applauded for limiting the Standards to the "what" and not mandating the "how." The classroom teacher will always be the best judge of how to meet his or her students' needs. But now that these Common Core Standards have been accepted, there will naturally be a learning curve for teachers to figure out how to use best practices in education to meet the new objectives.

Think of graphic organizers as your Common Core Standards superheroes that can swoop in to save the day! Because of the adaptability of graphic organizers, you can take any Standard, pair it with a reading selection, and create an effective lesson to meet that objective. It's easy to develop a top-notch reading lesson by choosing the right graphic organizer for the strategy or skill being taught.

In this chapter, I'll walk you through the process of designing a reading lesson. Then I'll explain how to use the graphic organizers in this book to meet Common Core Standards. The chapter continues with a step-by-step example: a lesson for introducing the Know-Wonder-Learned Chart to your students. At the end of Chapter 1 are charts for each grade, 2 - 6, that list the Common Core Reading Standards along with the graphic organizers you can use to teach them. You might be tempted to skip this chapter to dig into the graphic organizers in Chapters 2 and 3, but spending a few minutes reading this information could save you hours of planning time later. Let's get started!

Designing an Effective Reading Lesson

Creating an effective reading lesson is easier than you might think. My colleague Pat Calfee introduced me to a simple three-part process that takes the mystery out of lesson design. The entire process can be summarized in six words: "I Do, We Do, You Do."

This lesson framework is based on "gradual release of responsibility" and includes three stages, moving from teacher-directed instruction to independent work.

Possible components of each one of these stages are listed in the chart below. This three-stage progression can form the backbone of any reading lesson plan. It's a simple way for teachers to build reading lessons that will help their students learn and meet the Common Core Standards. The Reading Strategy Lesson Plan form on page 15 is your tool to help you develop lessons for literacy using the many graphic organizers in this book.

Lesson Phase	Lesson Components
I Do	**Teacher Input** ● Teacher introduces and explains the new strategy ● Teacher reads the text aloud ● Teacher "thinks aloud" to model how to apply the strategy ● Teacher demonstrates how to record thinking on a class anchor chart or with a graphic organizer
We Do	**Guided Practice** ● Students work with the teacher or with other students to practice the skill ● May take place in a whole group or a small group setting ● May involve partner work or cooperative learning activities ● Often involves analysis and discussion among class members
You Do	**Independent Practice** ● Students read independently and apply the new reading skill ● The reading text may be assigned by the teacher for a particular purpose or may be self-selected ● May involve written response in the form of journal writing or completion of a graphic organizer

Reading Strategy Lesson Plan

Targeted Strategies: _____

_____

Lesson Text(s): _____

Lesson Time Frame: _____

Graphic Organizer and/or Anchor Chart: _____

Lesson Plan	Lesson Outline
I DO Teacher Input	
WE DO Guided Practice	
YOU DO Independent Practice	

Chunking a Long Lesson into Mini-lessons

A complete reading lesson often lasts 45 minutes to an hour, especially when cooperative learning strategies are used during the lesson. However, many teachers want to teach reading "mini-lessons" that last no more than 20 minutes, to allow time for independent reading or learning centers. Does this mean that you need to squeeze the entire 3-part lesson into 20 minutes or less? Thankfully, the answer is a resounding "No!"

Learning to create mini-lessons simply means reevaluating lesson design. Instead of thinking of a lesson as the information you teach on a given day, consider a lesson as a sequence of instructional steps to teach a skill. Lessons aren't time-specific; when you're attuned to your students' needs and adapt your instruction accordingly, a lesson may take anywhere from a day to a week.

To create a reading mini-lesson from any complete lesson, simply chunk the full lesson into shorter segments. The "I Do, We Do, You Do" lesson sequence is the same, but it takes place over several days. You might begin on Day 1 with the "I Do" portion by reading part of your text aloud, explaining a strategy, and introducing a graphic organizer. Stop the lesson after 20 minutes to allow time for independent reading, small group work, or centers. The next day, pick the lesson back up with a quick review of the strategy followed by the "We Do" phase, as the students work with a partner. Once again, stop after 20 minutes to allow time for other reading activities. On the third day, wrap up the lesson by reviewing the strategy and asking students to read on their own and look for examples in their texts.

	How to Chunk a Full Lesson into Mini-lessons
DAY 1 (20 min.)	**I Do** Read aloud the selected text and introduce the skill with the corresponding graphic organizer. Ask your class for input as you work together to complete the graphic organizer. As you send your students off to read on their own, ask them to think about how they could apply the strategy, but don't require a written response since the strategy is new.
DAY 2 (20 min.)	**We Do** During the opening mini-lesson, ask your students to complete a blank graphic organizer with a partner. Walk around assisting and monitoring their progress. Then give each student another graphic organizer to begin using with an assigned text or their own self-selected book. They should be expected to add some details, but not to finish it that day.
DAY 3 (20 min.)	**You Do** During today's mini-lesson, review the strategy and ask students to share examples from their own books. Then send them off to read and allow plenty of class time for them to read independently and complete their own graphic organizers. When you are conferring with students individually, check their progress with the targeted skill.

Using Graphic Organizers to Meet Common Core Standards for Reading

Now you're ready to create your own reading lessons based on the Common Core Standards. These include 19 Reading Standards at each grade level: 10 for Informational Text and 9 for Literature. For every Common Core Standard in grades 2 through 6, there are one or more graphic organizers in this book to help you teach it. At the end of this chapter, starting on page 22, you'll find charts showing all of the Common Core Standards by grade level and at least one graphic organizer suggestion for each Standard. You may want to photocopy the chart for your grade level and keep it as a handy reference for lesson planning. The charts can also be downloaded at **www.lauracandler.com/gofr**.

Keep in mind that a graphic organizer alone does not make a reading lesson. If you remember the "I Do, We Do, You Do" lesson format, you'll know that creating an effective lesson involves much more than having students read a book and fill out a worksheet. Students must do more than take notes and write responses to literature; they must be given the opportunity to discuss the information, use what they've learned, make inferences, and draw conclusions.

To examine this concept more closely, let's look at how you can use a graphic organizer as a tool to teach a Standards-based lesson. The third grade Informational Text Reading Standard RI 3.5 states: "Use text features and search tools (e.g., key words, sidebars, hyperlinks) to locate information relevant to a given topic efficiently." Since this Standard is clearly dealing with Informational Text, flip to the chart on page 25 to find graphic organizers that are applicable. One choice for this Standard is the Informational Text Features Search graphic organizer (p. 87). Choose an appropriate text such as an encyclopedia or online article, duplicate a copy of the Informational Text Features Search for each student, and launch into your lesson. By the end of class, your students will be confidently finding and recording a variety of text features onto their charts.

But has your graphic organizer lesson actually met Common Core Standard RI 3.5? If you reread that Standard, you'll see that students have to *use* those text features "to locate information relevant to a given topic efficiently." Because the Standard also mentions key words and hyperlinks, you'll need to teach your students how to find information on the Internet. Luckily, there's another graphic organizer that can assist you in continuing your instruction on RI 3.5. The Research and Record graphic organizer on page 99 is the perfect tool to help students learn to research a favorite topic and record their findings.

Graphic organizers are teaching tools, and like any tool, they can be used and misused. In order to fully meet any single Standard, you may need to use several different graphic organizers and a variety of texts. Remember that developing these skills takes time, and your students will need multiple opportunities to apply their new skills in order to become proficient with each Standard.

Putting it All Together: Teaching a Common Core Standard Using a Graphic Organizer

Here is an example of a complete, step-by-step lesson plan for the Know-Wonder-Learned (KWL) Chart. The lesson description has not been chunked into mini-lessons, so you'll have to adapt it to your own time frame.

- **Common Core Standard: RI 3.1** – Ask and answer questions to demonstrate understanding of a text, referring explicitly to the text as the basis for the answers.
- **Text:** *Nature's Green Umbrella* by Gail Gibbons
- **Graphic Organizer:** Know-Wonder-Learned Chart (KWL)

The KWL chart is excellent for informational texts, and it can also be used with a literature selection if prior knowledge of a topic is key to understanding the story. This three-column graphic organizer requires students to list what they already know about a topic in the first column, and then pose questions that they wonder about in the second column. Finally, after they read or listen to the text, students return to the graphic organizer to record what they learned in the third column. The KWL chart is specifically aligned with the third grade Common Core Standard RI 3.1, but research has shown that activating prior knowledge before reading is important at any grade level.

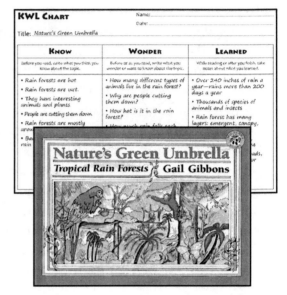

"I DO": Whole Class Modeling

1 Display a copy of the KWL chart on page 108 or draw a similar one on chart paper. If you wish, you can give your students their own copies and ask them to record details as you work on it together. However, this will slow the process considerably, so you may want to have them share ideas and watch you complete the class chart. Explain that good readers often think about what they already know about a topic, and then begin to wonder about what they'll learn while reading.

2 Ask your students what they know about tropical rain forests. To actively engage them, have students write their suggestions on individual dry-erase boards or slips of paper. As they offer ideas, record them in the

Know column. If they suggest a fact that's not correct, wait to see if anyone challenges the detail. If someone does question it, transfer the "fact" to the *Wonder* column. If no one challenges it, let the "fact" remain in the *Know* column; you can always move it later.

3 Ask your students what they wonder about the rain forest. Have students write their questions on dry-erase boards or on their own charts. Add as many of their questions to the *Wonder* column as time allows.

4 After you complete the *Know* and *Wonder* columns, read aloud *Nature's Green Umbrella,* being sure to show the illustrations as you read. Ask students to raise their hands if they hear the answer to a question, and then stop to record it on the chart. They can also record important information they learned, even if it's not the answer to a question. When introducing the graphic organizer as a part of a mini-lesson, you may need to finish the book the next day.

5 After you finish the book, ask the class to take a moment to review the chart. Are there any "facts" that need to be corrected? Are there any questions that have not been answered? If so, discuss how they might use other sources such as the Internet or other books to find the answers. However, let the students know that it's fine to leave some questions unanswered. If you require them to find the answer to every question, it may keep them from asking questions freely the next time they use the graphic organizer.

KWL Chart

Name: ....
Date: ....

Title: *Nature's Green Umbrella*

Know	Wonder	Learned
Before you read, write what you think you know about the topic.	Before or as you read, write what you wonder or want to know about this topic.	While reading or after you finish, take notes about what you learned.
• Rain forests are hot. • Rain forests are wet. • They have interesting animals and plants. • People are cutting them down. • Rain forests are mostly around the equator. • Bananas come from the rain forest.	• How many different types of animals live in the rain forest? • Why are people cutting them down? • How hot is it in the rain forest? • How much rain falls each year? • What products do we get from the rain forest?	• Over 240 inches of rain a year—rains more than 200 days a year • Thousands of species of animals and insects • Rain forest has many layers: emergent, canopy, understory, and floor • Products: fruits, nuts, vegetables, and medicine • Trees being cut for roads, lumber, clearing land for farming and mining

Laura's Tips

A document camera comes in handy when reading aloud books with interesting illustrations and diagrams.

"WE DO": Partner Practice

1 Pair students and assign them a different informational text to read together. Before they read, give them one blank KWL Chart to share between them and ask them to take turns adding facts to the **Know** column.

2 Ask them to write at least three or four questions in the **Wonder** column.

3 Ask them to read the book in whisper voices, taking turns on each paragraph or page. When they find an answer, they should stop to record it briefly. Remind them that they may record additional facts in that column, even if those facts are not the answer to a question. If they need more room to record notes, they can turn the paper over and continue writing what they learned on the back of the graphic organizer. In some cases, the partner practice step may take more than one day to complete.

"YOU DO": Independent Application

Students complete the KWL chart on their own with a short nonfiction book that they choose. If you are using the Reading Workshop approach, you may want them to use this graphic organizer instead of completing their usual reading response activity.

KWL Chart

Name: _____

Date: _____

Title: _Nature's Green Umbrella_

Know	Wonder	Learned
Before you read, write what you think you know about the topic.	Before or as you read, write what you wonder or want to know about the topic.	While reading or after you finish, take notes about what you learned.
• Rain forests are hot. • Rain forests are wet. • They have interesting animals and plants. • People are cutting them down. • Rain forests are mostly around the equator. • Bananas come from the rain forest.	• How many different types of animals live in the rain forest? • Why are people cutting them down? • How hot is it in the rain forest? • How much rain falls each year? • What products do we get from the rain forest?	• Over 240 inches of rain a year—rains more than 200 days a year • Thousands of species of animals and insects • Rain forest has many layers: emergent, canopy, understory, and floor • Products: fruits, nuts, vegetables, and medicine • Trees being cut for roads, lumber, clearing land for farming and mining

COMMON CORE STANDARDS   GRAPHIC ORGANIZERS TO USE

Key Ideas and Details

RL 2.1 Ask and answer such questions as *who, what, where, when, why,* and *how* to demonstrate understanding of key details in a text.	News Hound Summary (p. 110) T-chart (p. 40)
RL 2.2 Recount stories, including fables and folktales from diverse cultures, and determine their central message, lesson, or moral.	Literary Response Scroll (p. 144) News Hound Summary (p. 110)
RL 2.3 Describe how characters in a story respond to major events and challenges.	Cause and Effect Rockets (p. 115) Character Feelings Flow Map (p. 132)

Craft and Structure

RL 2.4 Describe how words and phrases (e.g., regular beats, alliteration, rhymes, repeated lines) supply rhythm and meaning in a story, poem, or song.	Poetry Peace Map (p. 146) Attribute Chart (p. 76)
RL 2.5 Describe the overall structure of a story, including describing how the beginning introduces the story and the ending concludes the action.	Story Plot Map (p. 139) Summarizing Sequencer (p. 134) Multi-column Chart (p. 44)
RL 2.6 Acknowledge differences in the points of view of characters, including by speaking in a different voice for each character when reading dialogue aloud.	T-chart (p. 40) Multi-column Chart (p. 44)

Integration of Knowledge and Ideas

RL 2.7 Use information gained from the illustrations and words in a print or digital text to demonstrate understanding of its characters, setting, or plot.	Story Map (p. 139) Story Plot Map (p. 139) Sequencing Strip (p. 66)
RL 2.8 (Not applicable to literature)	
RL 2.9 Compare and contrast two or more versions of the same story (e.g., Cinderella stories) by different authors or from different cultures.	Venn Diagram (p. 49)

Range of Reading and Level of Text Complexity

RL 2.10 By the end of the year, read and comprehend literature, including stories and poetry, in the grades 2–3 text complexity band proficiently, with scaffolding as needed at the high end of the range.	Literature Sharing Board (p. 70) Poetry Peace Map (p. 146) Poetic Reflections (p. 149) Literature Discussion Flapper (p. 64)

COMMON CORE STANDARDS	GRAPHIC ORGANIZERS TO USE
Key Ideas and Details	
RI 2.1 Ask and answer such questions as *who*, *what*, *where*, *when*, *why*, and *how* to demonstrate understanding of key details in a text.	News Hound Summary (p. 110)
RI 2.2 Identify the main topic of a multiparagraph text as well as the focus of specific paragraphs within the text.	Main Idea Neighborhood (p. 93)
RI 2.3 Describe the connection between a series of historical events, scientific ideas or concepts, or steps in technical procedures in a text.	Cause and Effect Rockets (p. 115) Sequencing Frames (p. 66)
Craft and Structure	
RI 2.4 Determine the meaning of words and phrases in a text relevant to a grade 2 topic or subject area.	Vocabulary Flapper (p. 112)
RI 2.5 Know and use various text features (e.g., captions, bold print, subheadings, glossaries, indexes, electronic menus, icons) to locate key facts or information in a text efficiently.	Informational Text Features Search (p. 87) Research and Record (p. 99)
RI 2.6 Identify the main purpose of a text, including what the author wants to answer, explain, or describe.	Main Idea Neighborhood (p. 93)
Integration of Knowledge and Ideas	
RI 2.7 Explain how specific images (e.g., a diagram showing how a machine works) contribute to and clarify a text.	Seeing Is Believing (p. 120)
RI 2.8 Describe how reasons support specific points the author makes in a text.	Folded Flapper (p. 58)
RI 2.9 Compare and contrast the most important points presented by two texts on the same topic.	Venn Diagram (p. 49)
Range of Reading and Level of Text Complexity	
RI 2.10 By the end of the year, read and comprehend informational texts, including history/social studies, science, and technical texts, in the grades 2–3 text complexity band proficiently, with scaffolding as needed at the high end of the range.	Informational Text Sharing Board (p. 70) Informational Text Discussion Flapper (p. 63) Research and Record (p. 99) Biographical Bits (p. 95)

COMMON CORE STANDARDS

GRAPHIC ORGANIZERS TO USE

Key Ideas and Details

Common Core Standards	Graphic Organizers to Use
RL 3.1 Ask and answer questions to demonstrate understanding of a text, referring explicitly to the text as the basis for the answers.	KWL Chart (p. 107) On Target Questions (p. 104) T-chart (p. 40)
RL 3.2 Recount stories, including fables, folktales, and myths from diverse cultures; determine the central message, lesson, or moral and explain how it is conveyed through key details in the text.	Literary Response Scroll (p. 144) Summarizing Sequencer (p. 134) Sequencing Frames (p. 67)
RL 3.3 Describe characters in a story (e.g., their traits, motivations, or feelings) and explain how their actions contribute to the sequence of events.	Character Trait Map (p. 123) Character Feelings Flow Map (p. 132) Cause and Effect Rockets (p. 115) Stick Figure Character Map (p. 128)

Craft and Structure

RL 3.4 Determine the meaning of words and phrases as they are used in a text, distinguishing literal from nonliteral language.	Attribute Chart (p. 76)
RL 3.5 Refer to parts of stories, dramas, and poems when writing or speaking about a text, using terms such as chapter, scene, and stanza; describe how each successive part builds on earlier sections.	Story Plot Map (p. 139) Poetic Reflections (p. 149)
RL 3.6 Distinguish their own point of view from that of the narrator or those of the characters.	Attribute Chart (p. 77)

Integration of Knowledge and Ideas

RL 3.7 Explain how specific aspects of a text's illustrations contribute to what is conveyed by the words in a story (e.g., create mood, emphasize aspects of a character or setting).	Seeing Is Believing (p. 120)
RL 3.8 (Not applicable to literature)	
RL 3.9 Compare and contrast the themes, settings, and plots of stories written by the same author about the same or similar characters (e.g., in books from a series).	Attribute Chart (p. 77)

Range of Reading and Complexity of Text

RL 3.10 By the end of the year, read and comprehend literature, including stories, dramas, and poetry, at the high end of the grades 2–3 text complexity band independently and proficiently.	Literature Sharing Board (p. 70) Poetry Peace Map (p. 146) Poetic Reflections (p. 149) Literature Discussion Flapper (p. 64)

COMMON CORE STANDARDS

GRAPHIC ORGANIZERS TO USE

Key Ideas and Details

RI 3.1 Ask and answer questions to demonstrate understanding of a text, referring explicitly to the text as the basis for the answers.	On Target Questions (p. 104)
RI 3.2 Determine the main idea of a text; recount the key details and explain how they support the main idea.	Main Idea Neighborhood (p. 93)
RI 3.3 Describe the relationship between a series of historical events, scientific ideas or concepts, or steps in technical procedures in a text, using language that pertains to time, sequence, and cause/effect.	Cause and Effect Rockets (p. 115) Sequencing Frames (p. 66)

Craft and Structure

RI 3.4 Determine the meaning of general academic and domain-specific words and phrases in a text relevant to a grade 3 topic or subject area.	Vocabulary Flapper (p. 112)
RI 3.5 Use text features and search tools (e.g., key words, sidebars, hyperlinks) to locate information relevant to a given topic efficiently.	Informational Text Features Search (p. 87) Research and Record (p. 99)
RI 3.6 Distinguish their own point of view from that of the author of a text.	Venn Diagram (p. 49)

Integration of Knowledge and Ideas

RI 3.7 Use information gained from illustrations (e.g., maps, photographs) and the words in a text to demonstrate understanding of the text (e.g., where, when, why, and how key events occur).	Seeing Is Believing (p. 120) On Target Questions (p. 104) News Hound Summary (p. 110)
RI 3.8 Describe the logical connection between particular sentences and paragraphs in a text (e.g., comparison, cause/effect, first/second/third in a sequence).	Informational Text Structures (p. 89) Cause and Effect Rockets (p. 115) Sequencing Frames (p. 67)
RI 3.9 Compare and contrast the most important points and key details presented in two texts on the same topic.	Venn Diagram (p. 49)

Range of Reading and Level of Text Complexity

RI 3.10 By the end of the year, read and comprehend informational texts, including history/social studies, science, and technical texts, at the high end of the grades 2–3 text complexity band independently and proficiently.	Informational Text Sharing Board (p. 70) Informational Text Discussion Flapper (p. 63) Research and Record (p. 99) Biographical Bits (p. 95)

COMMON CORE STANDARDS

GRAPHIC ORGANIZERS TO USE

Key Ideas and Details

RL 4.1 Refer to details and examples in a text when explaining what the text says explicitly and when drawing inferences from the text.	Step-by-Step Predictions (p. 142) Stick Figure Character Map (p. 128)
RL 4.2 Determine a theme of a story, drama, or poem from details in the text; summarize the text.	Literary Response Scroll (p. 144) Poetry Peace Map (p. 146) Poetic Reflections (p. 149) Summarizing Sequencer (p. 134)
RL 4.3 Describe in depth a character, setting, or event in a story or drama, drawing on specific details in the text (e.g., a character's thoughts, words, or actions).	Stick Figure Character Map (p. 128) Character Trait Map (p. 123) Multi-column Chart (p. 44) Folded Flapper (p. 58)

Craft and Structure

RL 4.4 Determine the meaning of words and phrases as they are used in a text, including those that allude to significant characters found in mythology (e.g., Herculean).	Vocabulary Flapper (p. 112) Attribute Chart (p. 76)
RL 4.5 Explain major differences between poems, drama, and prose, and refer to the structural elements of poems (e.g., verse, rhythm, meter) and drama (e.g., casts of characters, settings, descriptions, dialogue, stage directions) when writing or speaking about a text.	Attribute Chart (p. 77) Venn Diagram (p. 49)
RL 4.6 Compare and contrast the point of view from which different stories are narrated, including the difference between first- and third-person narrations.	Attribute Chart (p. 77)

Integration of Knowledge and Ideas

RL 4.7 Make connections between the text of a story or drama and a visual or oral presentation of the text, identifying where each version reflects specific descriptions and directions in the text.	T-chart (p. 40)
RL 4.8 (Not applicable to literature)	
RL 4.9 Compare and contrast the treatment of similar themes and topics (e.g., opposition of good and evil) and patterns of events (e.g., the quest) in stories, myths, and traditional literature from different cultures.	Attribute Chart (p. 77)

Range of Reading and Complexity of Text

RL 4.10 By the end of the year, read and comprehend literature, including stories, dramas, and poetry, in the grades 4–5 text complexity band proficiently, with scaffolding as needed at the high end of the range.	Literature Sharing Board (p. 70) Poetry Peace Map (p. 146) Poetic Reflections (p. 149) Literature Discussion Flapper (p. 64)

COMMON CORE STANDARDS

GRAPHIC ORGANIZERS TO USE

Key Ideas and Details

Common Core Standards	Graphic Organizers to Use
RI 4.1 Refer to details and examples in a text when explaining what the text says explicitly and when drawing inferences from the text.	It All Adds Up (p. 117) T-chart (p. 40)
RI 4.2 Determine the main idea of a text and explain how it is supported by key details; summarize the text.	Main Idea Neighborhood (p. 93)
RI 4.3 Explain events, procedures, ideas, or concepts in a historical, scientific, or technical text, including what happened and why, based on specific information in the text.	Sequencing Frames (p. 67) News Hound Summary (p. 110)

Craft and Structure

Common Core Standards	Graphic Organizers to Use
RI 4.4 Determine the meaning of general academic and domain-specific words or phrases in a text relevant to a grade 4 topic or subject area.	Vocabulary Flapper (p. 112)
RI 4.5 Describe the overall structure (e.g., chronology, comparison, cause/effect, problem/solution) of events, ideas, concepts, or information in a text or part of a text.	Informational Text Structures (p. 89)
RI 4.6 Compare and contrast a firsthand and secondhand account of the same event or topic; describe the differences in focus and the information provided.	Venn Diagram (p. 49)

Integration of Knowledge and Ideas

Common Core Standards	Graphic Organizers to Use
RI 4.7 Interpret information presented visually, orally, or quantitatively (e.g., in charts, graphs, diagrams, time lines, animations, or interactive elements on Web pages) and explain how the information contributes to an understanding of the text in which it appears.	Seeing Is Believing (p. 120)
RI 4.8 Explain how an author uses reasons and evidence to support particular points in a text.	Folded Flapper (p. 58)
RI 4.9 Integrate information from two texts on the same topic in order to write or speak about the subject knowledgeably.	Research and Record (p. 99) Biographical Bits (p. 95) T-chart (p. 40)

Range of Reading and Level of Text Complexity

Common Core Standards	Graphic Organizers to Use
RI 4.10 By the end of year, read and comprehend informational texts, including history/social studies, science, and technical texts, in the grades 4–5 text complexity band proficiently, with scaffolding as needed at the high end of the range.	Informational Text Sharing Board (p. 70) Informational Text Discussion Flapper (p. 63) Research and Record (p. 99) Biographical Bits (p. 95)

COMMON CORE STANDARDS

GRAPHIC ORGANIZERS TO USE

Key Ideas and Details

Common Core Standards	Graphic Organizers to Use
RL 5.1 Quote accurately from a text when explaining what the text says explicitly and when drawing inferences from the text.	Step-by-Step Predictions (p. 142) It All Adds Up (p. 117) T-chart (p. 40)
RL 5.2 Determine a theme of a story, drama, or poem from details in the text, including how characters in a story or drama respond to challenges or how the speaker in a poem reflects upon a topic; summarize the text.	Literary Response Scroll (p. 144) Summarizing Sequencer (p. 134) Poetry Peace Map (p. 146) Poetic Reflections (p. 149)
RL 5.3 Compare and contrast two or more characters, settings, or events in a story or drama, drawing on specific details in the text (e.g., how characters interact).	Venn Diagram (p. 50)

Craft and Structure

Common Core Standards	Graphic Organizers to Use
RL 5.4 Determine the meaning of words and phrases as they are used in a text, including figurative language such as metaphors and similes.	Folded Flapper (p. 58)
RL 5.5 Explain how a series of chapters, scenes, or stanzas fits together to provide the overall structure of a particular story, drama, or poem.	Story Plot Map (p. 139) Attribute Chart (p. 77)
RL 5.6 Describe how a narrator's or speaker's point of view influences how events are described.	Attribute Chart (p. 78)

Integration of Knowledge and Ideas

Common Core Standards	Graphic Organizers to Use
RL 5.7 Analyze how visual and multimedia elements contribute to the meaning, tone, or beauty of a text (e.g., graphic novel, multimedia presentation of fiction, folktale, myth, poem).	Seeing Is Believing (p. 120)
RL 5.8 (Not applicable to literature)	
RL 5.9 Compare and contrast stories in the same genre (e.g., mysteries and adventure stories) on their approaches to similar themes and topics.	Attribute Chart (p. 78)

Range of Reading and Complexity of Text

Common Core Standards	Graphic Organizers to Use
RL 5.10 By the end of the year, read and comprehend literature, including stories, dramas, and poetry, at the high end of the grades 4–5 text complexity band independently and proficiently.	Literature Sharing Board (p. 70) Poetry Peace Map (p. 146) Poetic Reflections (p. 149) Literature Discussion Flapper (p. 64)

COMMON CORE STANDARDS

GRAPHIC ORGANIZERS TO USE

Key Ideas and Details

RI 5.1 Quote accurately from a text when explaining what the text says explicitly and when drawing inferences from the text.	It All Adds Up (p. 117)
RI 5.2 Determine two or more main ideas of a text and explain how they are supported by key details; summarize the text.	Main Idea Neighborhood (p. 93)
RI 5.3 Explain the relationships or interactions between two or more individuals, events, ideas, or concepts in a historical, scientific, or technical text based on specific information in the text.	Research and Record (p. 99) Biographical Bits (p. 95) Cause and Effect Rockets (p. 115)

Craft and Structure

RI 5.4 Determine the meaning of general academic and domain-specific words and phrases in a text relevant to a grade 5 topic or subject area.	Vocabulary Flapper (p. 112)
RI 5.5 Compare and contrast the overall structure (e.g., chronology, comparison, cause/effect, problem/solution) of events, ideas, concepts, or information in two or more texts.	Informational Text Structures (p. 89)
RI 5.6 Analyze multiple accounts of the same event or topic, noting important similarities and differences in the point of view they represent.	Venn Diagram (p. 50)

Integration of Knowledge and Ideas

RI 5.7 Draw on information from multiple print or digital sources, demonstrating the ability to locate an answer to a question quickly or to solve a problem efficiently.	KWL Chart (p. 107) On Target Questions (p. 104) Research and Record (p. 99) Multi-column Chart (p. 44)
RI 5.8 Explain how an author uses reasons and evidence to support particular points in a text, identifying which reasons and evidence support which point(s).	Multi-column Chart (p. 44)
RI 5.9 Integrate information from several texts on the same topic in order to write or speak about the subject knowledgeably.	Research and Record (p. 99) Biographical Bits (p. 95) Multi-column Chart (p. 44)

Range of Reading and Level of Text Complexity

RI 5.10 By the end of the year, read and comprehend informational texts, including history/social studies, science, and technical texts, at the high end of the grades 4–5 text complexity band independently and proficiently.	Informational Text Sharing Board (p. 70) Informational Text Discussion Flapper (p. 63) Research and Record (p. 99) Biographical Bits (p. 95)

COMMON CORE STANDARDS	GRAPHIC ORGANIZERS TO USE
Key Ideas and Details	
RL 6.1 Cite textual evidence to support analysis of what the text says explicitly as well as inferences drawn from the text.	Step-by-Step Predictions (p. 142) T-chart (p. 40) Attribute Chart (p. 78)
RL 6.2 Determine a theme or central idea of a text and how it is conveyed through particular details; provide a summary of the text distinct from personal opinions or judgments.	Literary Response Scroll (p. 144) Summarizing Sequencer (p. 134)
RL 6.3 Describe how a particular story's or drama's plot unfolds in a series of episodes as well as how the characters respond or change as the plot moves toward a resolution.	Sequencing Frames (p. 67) Story Plot Map (p. 139)
Craft and Structure	
RL 6.4 Determine the meaning of words and phrases as they are used in a text, including figurative and connotative meanings; analyze the impact of a specific word choice on meaning and tone.	Attribute Chart (p. 78)
RL 6.5 Analyze how a particular sentence, chapter, scene, or stanza fits into the overall structure of a text and contributes to the development of the theme, setting, or plot.	Folded Flapper (p. 58) Attribute Chart (p. 78)
RL 6.6 Explain how an author develops the point of view of the narrator or speaker in a text.	Sequencing Frames (p. 67)
Integration of Knowledge and Ideas	
RL 6.7 Compare and contrast the experience of reading a story, drama, or poem to listening to or viewing an audio, video, or live version of the text, including contrasting what they "see" and "hear" when reading the text to what they perceive when they listen or watch.	Venn Diagram (p. 50)
RL 6.8 (Not applicable to literature)	
RL 6.9 Compare and contrast texts in different forms or genres (e.g., stories and poems; historical novels and fantasy stories) in terms of their approaches to similar themes and topics.	Attribute Chart (p. 78)
Range of Reading and Level of Text Complexity	
RL 6.10 By the end of the year, read and comprehend literature, including stories, dramas, and poems, in the grades 6–8 text complexity band proficiently, with scaffolding as needed at the high end of the range.	Literature Sharing Board (p. 70) Poetry Peace Map (p. 146) Poetic Reflections (p. 149) Literature Discussion Flapper (p. 64)

COMMON CORE STANDARDS

GRAPHIC ORGANIZERS TO USE

Key Ideas and Details

Common Core Standards	Graphic Organizers to Use
RI 6.1 Cite textual evidence to support analysis of what the text says explicitly as well as inferences drawn from the text.	Step-by-Step Predictions (p. 142) It All Adds Up (p. 117) T-chart (p. 40)
RI 6.2 Determine a central idea of a text and how it is conveyed through particular details; provide a summary of the text distinct from personal opinions or judgments.	Main Idea Neighborhood (p. 93)
RI 6.3 Analyze in detail how a key individual, event, or idea is introduced, illustrated, and elaborated in a text (e.g., through examples or anecdotes).	Sequencing Frames (p. 67)

Craft and Structure

RI 6.4 Determine the meaning of words and phrases as they are used in a text, including figurative, connotative, and technical meanings.	Vocabulary Flapper (p. 112)
RI 6.5 Analyze how a particular sentence, paragraph, chapter, or section fits into the overall structure of a text and contributes to the development of the ideas.	Informational Text Structures (p. 89)
RI 6.6 Determine an author's point of view or purpose in a text and explain how it is conveyed in the text.	Sequencing Frames (p. 67)

Integration of Knowledge and Ideas

RI 6.7 Integrate information presented in different media or formats (e.g., visually, quantitatively) as well as in words to develop a coherent understanding of a topic or issue.	Research and Record (p. 99) Multi-column Chart (p. 44)
RI 6.8 Trace and evaluate the argument and specific claims in a text, distinguishing claims that are supported by reasons and evidence from claims that are not.	Sequencing Frames (p. 67)
RI 6.9 Compare and contrast one author's presentation of events with that of another (e.g., a memoir written by and a biography on the same person).	Venn Diagram (p. 50)

Range of Reading and Level of Text Complexity

RI 6.10 By the end of the year, read and comprehend literary nonfiction in the grades 6–8 text complexity band proficiently, with scaffolding as needed at the high end of the range.	Informational Text Sharing Board (p. 70) Informational Text Discussion Flapper (p. 63) Research and Record (p. 99) Biographical Bits (p. 95)

CHAPTER 2

Multi-purpose Graphic Organizers

Multi-purpose Graphic Organizers

• • • • • • • • • •

Multi-purpose graphic organizers are incredibly versatile teaching tools. The number of ways you can use them is limited only by your imagination. After you understand how they work, it's easy to decide which graphic organizer is best for any type of text. Most of them can be used with both informational text and literature, and quite a few of them are appropriate for a wide range of content areas. This chapter has seven multi-purpose graphic organizers with directions for how to use each one, including a sample lesson. Printer-friendly versions of some of the graphic organizers can be downloaded at **www.lauracandler.com/ gofr**. Those organizers have the "online" icon at the bottom of the page.

Each graphic organizer includes its "Common Core Connections," a section that shows how to use the graphic organizer to teach a variety of specific Common Core Standards.

Multi-purpose Graphic Organizers:

The seven multi-purpose graphic organizers in this chapter are presented in a logical sequence from the simplest to the most complex. You may introduce them in any order you prefer, but if your students have not had any prior experience with these graphic organizers, you may want to follow the sequence below.

- T-charts
- Multi-column Charts
- Venn Diagrams
- Folded Flappers
- Sequencing Frames
- Sharing Boards
- Attribute Charts

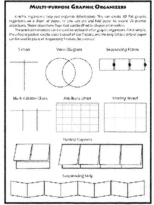

Introducing New Graphic Organizers

When you first introduce a new graphic organizer to your students, I recommend applying it to a non-academic concept or something personally relevant. I call these "fun" introductions. For example, when you first introduce a Venn diagram, you could have your students compare two popular movies or two comic book characters. These activities serve as great team builders while teaching your students the essential elements of the graphic organizer.

As you use different graphic organizers throughout the year, explain to your students why you have chosen each one and ask them for their ideas. For example, some organizers are more suited to comparison while others may be better for sequencing events. Try to use the graphic organizers with both literature and informational text selections so that students can see how the same one can be used in many ways.

Laura's Tips

Be sure to save graphic organizer examples throughout the year. You can ask students to donate their graphic organizers to your collection after each lesson or photograph their work with a digital camera. Later, you can refer to these examples when teaching students how to choose the best organizer for a particular text.

Teaching Students to Choose the Best Graphic Organizer

When you feel your students are ready to begin choosing their own graphic organizers, you can use the lesson below. You may want to give them a copy of the Multi-purpose Graphic Organizer chart on page 38 to keep in their notebooks to use as a reference when they are trying to figure out which multi-purpose graphic organizer will work best.

1 DISPLAY AND DISCUSS GRAPHIC ORGANIZERS ● Prior to this lesson, you should have introduced your students to all of the multi-purpose graphic organizers. Display the examples you have saved from previous lessons, and review why each graphic organizer was selected for a particular text type.

2 DISCUSS DIFFERENCES IN TEXT TYPES ● Introducing the Informational Text Structures graphic organizer on page 89 prior to this lesson is helpful because that lesson gives students a basic understanding of the different types of informational texts. Ask them to think about how informational text structures are different from literary text structures:

● Literature selections usually involve characters, setting, and plot. The events usually take place in chronological order.

● Informational texts may be organized in other ways, such as by main idea and details, cause and effect, sequence of events, question and answer, and so on.

3 MATCH GRAPHIC ORGANIZERS WITH TEXTS ● Ask students to look at the multi-purpose graphic organizer examples on page 38 and determine which of them would work best with informational texts, and which would work best with literature. Some of them can easily be used with both.

4 LET STUDENTS CHOOSE ● When possible, from this point forward, allow students to choose the folded or flat graphic organizer that best meets their needs. Ask them to justify their choices to a partner or small group before starting to work on their graphic organizer. You might even choose to have them turn over their graphic organizer and write their reason for choosing it on the back.

MULTI-PURPOSE GRAPHIC ORGANIZERS

Graphic organizers help you organize information. You can create 2D flat graphic organizers on a sheet of paper, or you can cut and fold paper to create 3D graphic organizers. These often have flaps that can be lifted to display information.

These folded variations can be used to replace the flat graphic organizers. For example, the 2-flap organizer can be used instead of the T-chart, and the long folded strip of paper can be used in place of Sequencing Frames. Be creative!

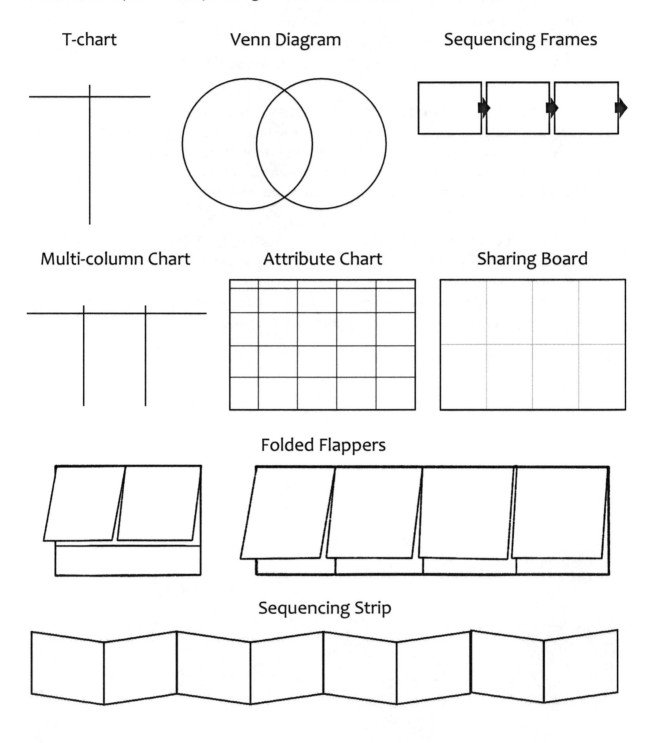

T-chart   Venn Diagram   Sequencing Frames

Multi-column Chart   Attribute Chart   Sharing Board

Folded Flappers

Sequencing Strip

T-charts

The T-chart is the simplest graphic organizer: two columns labeled with topic headers. T-charts are used to organize information as it is recorded. Teachers frequently use T-charts to create "anchor charts" during reading mini-lessons. As they read and discuss a particular text with the class, they record details on an anchor chart that can be saved and used as a reference during a future lesson.

Fun Introduction:
List the pros and cons of homework

Ask your students to think about the pros and cons of doing homework. Create a large class T-chart to use during your discussion. Ask students to write each pro or con of homework on a sticky note and post them on the chart. Challenge your students to find an equal number of pros and cons.

Purposes

● Sort and classify concepts into two categories

● Identify two sides of an issue

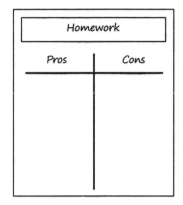

Sample Lesson: Fact and Opinion

A T-chart makes an easy way to list facts and opinions found in a reading selection.

1 Display the chart on page 41 or draw a T-chart on the board.

2 Ask students to draw a similar chart on their own paper.

3 Read aloud from an informational article, a book, or a website that includes clear examples of facts and opinions. As you read aloud, ask students to raise their hands when they hear a fact or an opinion. Discuss each statement before having students jot it down on their own charts or before writing it on the class chart.

4 Remind students that facts can be verified by measuring, counting, or using reliable sources of data. Opinions tell what someone thinks and frequently include evaluative words like "should," "best," or "worst." The example on page 42 is based on the rain forest, a topic with an abundance of facts and opinions.

5 After they practice the skill as a class, give them another text to practice with a partner. Ask students to take turns writing facts and opinions on their chart and provide time for sharing their results with the class at the end of the lesson.

Common Core Connections

RL 2.1, RL 3.1 – Use a T-chart to help students ask and answer questions to demonstrate understanding of key details in a text. List questions before reading a book on the left side, and record answers or information learned on the right side.

RL 2.6 – To analyze character point of view, write two character names at the top of the T-chart as headings. Then list details that give the reader clues about their points of view in the columns under their names.

RL 4.7 – Create a T-chart to compare a written text with a visual, dramatic, or oral version of the same text. Title one column **Written Text** and the other **Presentation**, and list details showing the connections between the two. Identify where each version reflects specific descriptions and directions in the text.

RI 4.1, RL 5.1, RI 6.1, RL 6.1 – Use a T-chart to note where a text states something explicitly and where inferences must be drawn. For the column headings, write **Stated in the Text**, and **My Inferences**. List details from the text and inferences from the text accordingly.

RI 4.9 – Use a T-chart to integrate information from two texts on the same topic in order to write or speak about the subject knowledgeably. Select two texts that are on the same topic, write the titles as column headings, and take notes under each heading. Use the notes as the basis for a written and/or oral report.

FACT AND OPINION T-CHART

Topic ➡ [   ]

Facts	Opinions

FACT AND OPINION

Topic Tropical Rain Forests

Facts	Opinions
• Rain forests receive over 240 inches of rain a year.	• The Amazon Rain Forest is the most beautiful place on earth.
• It rains more than 200 days every year.	• People who live in the rain forests shouldn't cut down the trees to clear land for roads and homes.
• Thousands of species of animals and insects live in the rain forest.	• Hunting animals to sell for their fur is wrong.
• The tropical rain forest has many layers, such as the emergent layer, canopy, understory, and forest floor.	• Destruction of tropical rain forests is one of our biggest environmental challenges.
• Products from the rain forest include fruits, nuts, vegetables, and medicine.	• The sweetest pineapples come from the tropical rain forest.
• Trees are being cut down for roads, lumber, farming, and mining.	• Big companies are greedy when they cut down the trees to make room for cattle farms.
• Astronauts in space can see smoke from rain forest fires.	

Multi-column Charts

After you've introduced the T-chart, it's simple to create a multi-column chart by adding a column or two. There's no need to print out this graphic organizer because it's so easy to draw, but a blank template is provided for you to display for the class or duplicate if desired. If students are drawing them on letter-sized paper, you probably don't want more than three columns because the columns become very narrow. If you need more columns, use legal-sized paper or posterboard.

Purposes

- Take notes or list details

- Classify concepts under multiple subtopics or categories

Fun Introduction:
What's Your Favorite Food?

Draw a 3-column chart on your blackboard or on chart paper, and title it *Favorite Foods*. Call on at least 10 volunteers to each add one favorite food to the chart in the appropriate column of breakfast, lunch, or dinner, creating bulleted lists of foods in the columns. Remind students that they don't have to write in complete sentences when they are listing items or taking notes.

FAVORITE FOODS		
Breakfast	Lunch	Dinner

Sample Lesson: News Review

The News Review graphic organizer (p. 46) is an effective way to use a three-column chart. The example on page 47 was based on an article about an emu on the loose.

1 Find an interesting local news article or use the emu article if it's available online (http://www.fayobserver.com/articles/2012/01/05/1147597).

2 Display the blank graphic organizer and ask students to help you find the important facts and details (the *who, what, where, when, why,* and *how* of the news story). As they identify relevant details, list them on the chart.

3 Ask students why the information in the article is newsworthy. Why is it important? List their ideas in the middle column.

4 Ask volunteers to share their personal responses, which might include unanswered questions, their feelings about the topic, connections, inferences, or even predictions about how the story will turn out.

5 After they understand how to use the graphic organizer, have students read a different article with a partner and complete another News Review together.

Common Core Connections

RL 2.5 – Create a multi-column chart with the headings *Beginning, Middle*, and *End*. As you read a story, list the important details under each heading.

RL 2.6 – To analyze character point of view, write several character names at the top of a multi-column chart as headings. Then list details that give the readers clues about their points of view in the columns under their names.

RL 4.3 – To describe a character in depth, create a multi-column chart with the headings *Character Thoughts, Character Words*, and *Character Action*s. List specific supporting details from the story or drama in the columns under each heading.

RI 5.7 – To demonstrate the ability to locate and answer a question or solve a problem from multiple sources, create a multi-column chart on a single topic with the digital or print sources listed at the top of each column. Under the column headings, list the types of information that are available in that source. Use the chart as a resource when attempting to find an answer or solve a problem about that topic.

RI 5.8 – To identify the reasons and evidence that an author uses to support particular points in a text, create a multi-column chart. For headings at the top of the chart, write brief statements summarizing various points that the author is making in the text. Under each statement, write details that include reasons and evidence the author cites to support that point. Refer to the chart when explaining how an author uses reasons and evidence to support particular points in a text.

RI 5.9 – To integrate information from several texts on the same topic, create a multi-column chart on one topic. Select several texts related to that topic and write their titles as the column headers. While reading each text, take notes under the appropriate column header. Use the chart as a reference to write or speak about the subject knowledgably.

RI 6.7 – To integrate information from several media or formats, create a multi-column chart and title it with the topic or issue. Select several sources that present the information in different media or formats, and write the title of each source as column headers. Directly under each header, notate the type of media or format. While reading and researching, take notes under the appropriate column header. Use the chart as a reference to develop a coherent understanding of the topic.

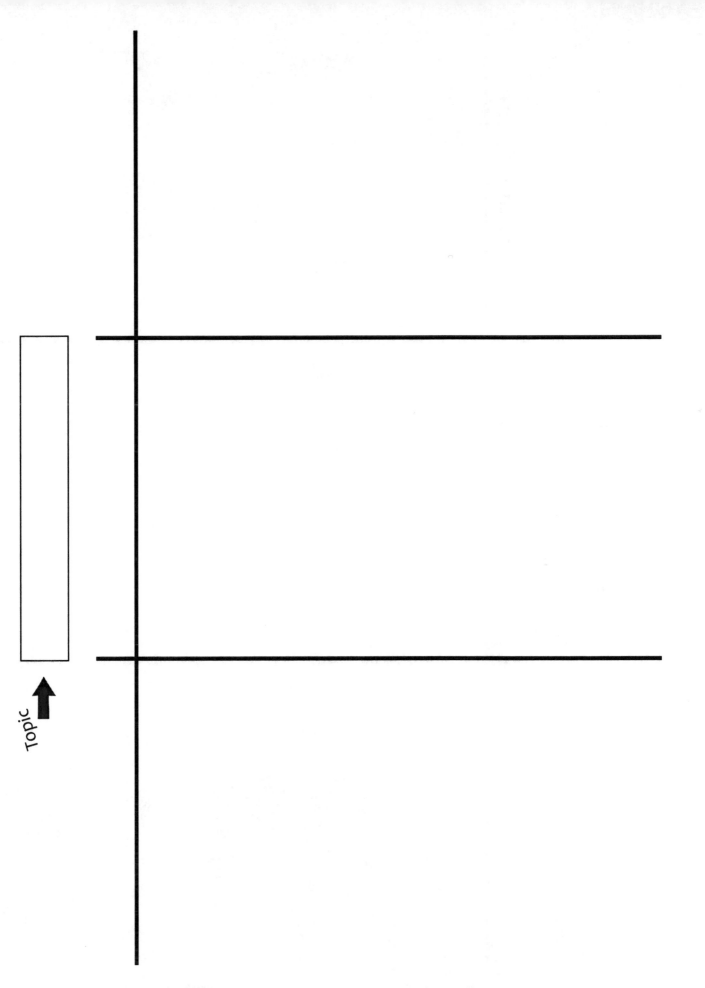

Topic

News Review

Name: _____

Title: _____

Article Date: _____

Source: _____

Facts & Details	Why Important?	Personal Response

News Review

Name: _Sally Jones_

Article Date: _January 5, 2012_

Title: _6-foot tall Emu Roaming Harnett County Countryside_ Source: _Fayetteville Observer Newspaper_

Facts & Details

- Emu seen by 8 people in Harnett County, NC

- Emu is 6 feet tall, flightless bird common to Australia

- Eats nuts, berries, and bugs

- Imported in 1930s for meat & leathery skin

- Has sharp claws that can hurt people

- Emu hasn't threatened any- one so far

- No plans to trap emu

- Last emu captured in NC died in captivity

Why Important?

- Emus are not usually seen in NC so people need to know this information in case they see it

- Emus can be dangerous when threatened

- If people see an emu, they need to know that it could be dangerous so they won't try to capture it

Personal Response

- It was funny when the emu was looking in the window and the lady said she thought it was the biggest turkey she had ever seen!

- I wonder where the emu came from and how long it's been on the loose?

- I wonder if the emu could survive our winter weather?

- I hope the emu stays free because I think it would be sad for it be captured and maybe die in captivity.

Venn Diagrams

A Venn diagram offers a way to compare two or more topics that have both similarities and differences. Venn diagrams are the next logical step after introducing T-charts and multi-column charts because they require students to consider the relationships between ideas rather than simply listing details for each topic individually. Almost any Common Core Standard that includes the words "compare and contrast" can be taught by using a Venn diagram to organize information prior to a discussion or writing assignment. After students become proficient with using a two-circle Venn diagram, you can introduce them to the three-circle Venn diagram.

Purpose

● Compare and contrast related topics

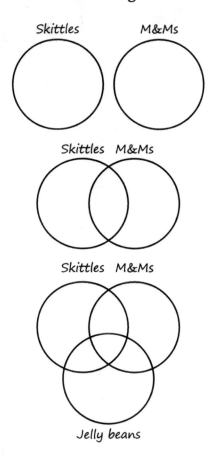

Fun Introduction:
Characteristics of Skittles and M&Ms

Draw two large circles that don't overlap and write "Skittles" above one circle and "M&Ms" above the other. Give each student a few pieces of each type of candy and ask them to name characteristics of these candies. As they do so, write the details on sticky notes and place them in the two circles. Soon they will begin naming characteristics that both candies have in common, such as being colorful and sweet. Show your students that if you move the circles together and overlap them, they only need to write those characteristics once and place them in the overlapping area. When students are ready, you can add a third candy with a third overlapping circle to illustrate how a Venn diagram can compare more than two things.

LAURA'S Tips

If you have two or three large Hula-Hoops, you can place them on the floor and ask students to sit in a circle around them.

Sample Lesson: Comparing Text Types

A Venn diagram is an excellent tool to use when comparing and contrasting informational texts and literature.

1 Gather a collection of both informational texts and literature, and ask students to look through them to find examples of text structures and features that differentiate the two genres.

2 Have students work with a partner on a shared Venn diagram and then add details to create a class chart such as the one on page 52. Remind them that these details are general characteristics and don't hold true for every informational text or literature selection.

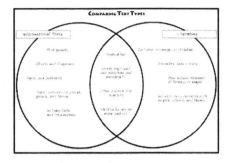

Common Core Connections

RI 2.9, RL 2.9 – Compare and contrast two or more versions of the same story or two books on the same topic.

RI 3.6 – Create a Point of View Venn diagram based on an informational selection about a topic. Write **My Point of View** at the top of the right circle and **Author's Point of View** at the top of the left circle. In the right circle, list details to describe your own point of view. In the left circle, include both the author's point of view and the text or visual details that provide clues to determining his or her point of view.

RI 3.9 – When researching a topic, read two informational texts on a single topic and create a topic-specific Venn diagram to compare and contrast the information. Each circle will be titled with the name of one text; record facts and details in the appropriate places on the graphic organizer.

RL 4.5 – Create a large, three-circle Venn diagram to explore major differences between poems, drama, and prose. Head each circle with **Drama**, **Poetry**, and **Prose**. As you review the characteristics of each, refer to their structural elements (e.g., verse, rhythm, meter, characters, settings, descriptions, dialogue, stage directions) and list details accordingly.

RI 4.6 – When reading about an event, compare and contrast a firsthand and secondhand account of the same event or topic. Create a Venn diagram with two circles titled **Firsthand Account** and **Secondhand Account**; in each circle, list details that describe the differences in focus and the information provided.

RL 5.3 – Use a Venn diagram to compare and contrast two or more characters, settings, or events in a story or drama, listing specific details in the text in each circle.

RI 5.6 – Use a two- or three-circle Venn diagram to analyze multiple accounts of the same event or topic. Be sure to note important similarities and differences in the point of view they represent.

RL 6.7 – Create a Venn diagram to compare and contrast the experience of reading a story, drama, or poem to listening to or viewing an audio, video, or live version of the text. Label the two circles *Written Text* and *Performance*. In each circle, include details contrasting what they "see" and "hear" when reading the text to what they see and hear when they listen or watch the performance.

RI 6.9 – Create a Venn diagram to compare and contrast one author's presentation of events with that of another (e.g., a memoir written by and a biography on the same person).

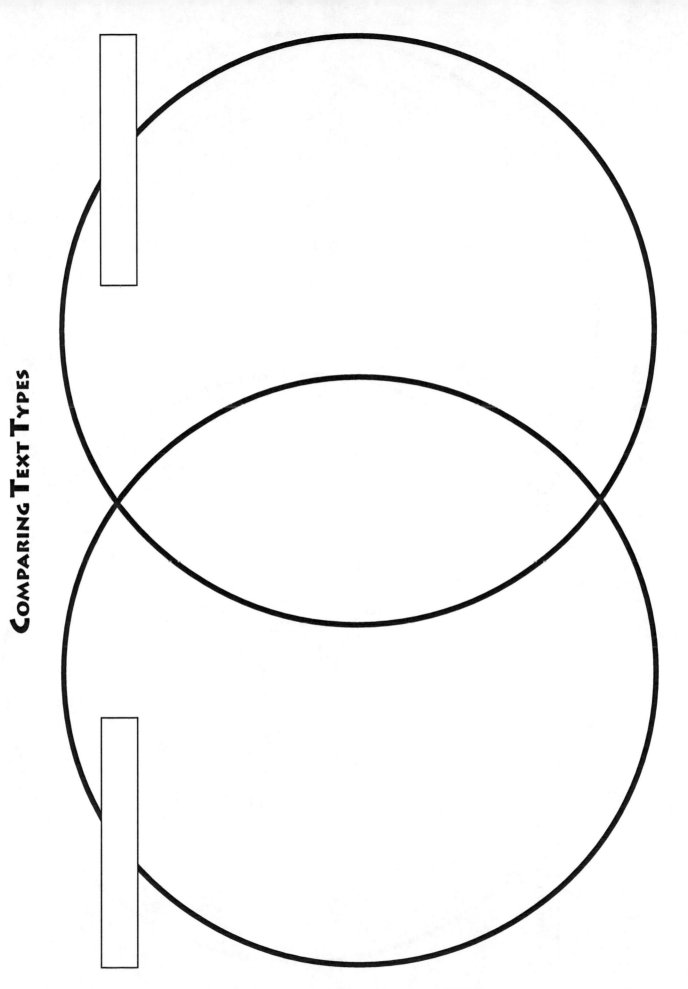

COMPARING TEXT TYPES

COMPARING TEXT TYPES

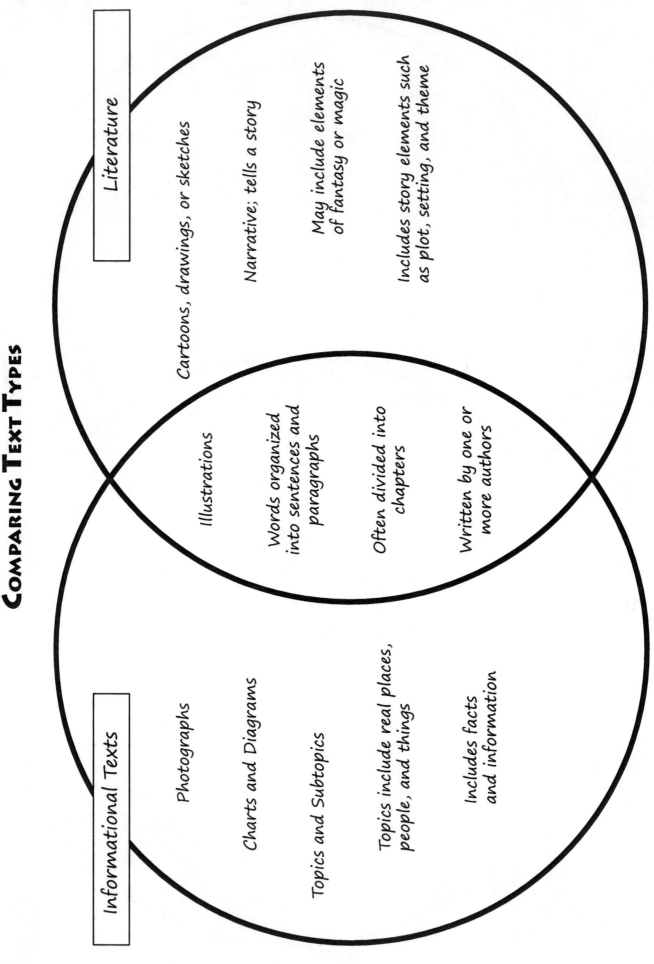

Literature

Cartoons, drawings, or sketches

Narrative; tells a story

May include elements of fantasy or magic

Includes story elements such as plot, setting, and theme

Illustrations

Words organized into sentences and paragraphs

Often divided into chapters

Written by one or more authors

Informational Texts

Photographs

Charts and Diagrams

Topics and Subtopics

Topics include real places, people, and things

Includes facts and information

Folded Flappers

Folded flappers (or just "flappers") are folded graphic organizers with flaps. Kids love to cut and fold paper, and having them create flappers is a great way to tap into their creativity.

Flat organizers or flappers? They're often interchangeable. Two-flap graphic organizers can easily replace T-charts, and long skinny flappers can be created instead of using multi-column charts.

The KWL chart (page 108) is a flat graphic organizer that can be replaced with a folded one. Since the chart has three columns, it's easy to substitute a three-flap folded graphic organizer. Notice how each column heading becomes a heading on the corresponding flap.

Flappers have several advantages over flat ones. They don't require photocopying, and the flapper can easily be folded and tucked inside a book to save for later. Creating the folded version also gives students practice in following directions and engages the kinesthetic learner.

How can you decide whether to use a flat graphic organizer or a folded one? Part of your decision may be based on the amount of time you have for the activity. Flappers do take more time to create than flat graphic organizers, but they can be more fun for kids. At first, use a pattern that shows them where to fold and cut the page. Eventually your students will be able to create their own flappers from plain paper in a matter of minutes.

Purposes

● Take notes

● Record literature responses

● Organize information into categories

● Compare and contrast concepts

Laura's Tips

At first, it's more time-consuming to have students create folded graphic organizers. But after students learn how to make them, they delight in quickly folding and cutting a piece of paper to use in a lesson.

Two-Part Flappers

This simple two-flap graphic organizer is an easy way to introduce your students to flappers. Begin by having your students use the pattern on page 56 the first time. After that, they can use the directions on page 55 to create one from blank paper.

Fun Introduction:
Comparing School Calendars

Start by choosing a somewhat controversial topic that interests your class. For example, many school systems have debated the benefits of a year-round calendar versus the traditional calendar with summers off. Have students create a two-part flapper called **School Calendars**. As your class discusses the pros and cons of each type of calendar, list the details in the space under each flap, labeled **Year-Round** and **Traditional**.

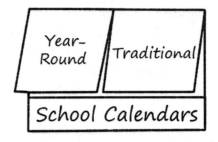

Sample Lesson - Research and Note-Taking

The two-part graphic organizer makes a great note-taking flapper that students can tuck into a book.

One topic that fascinates many students is how people traveled in wagon trains during the 1800s. *The Wagon Train* by Bobbie Kalman includes illustrations and facts about life on a wagon train, and it makes an excellent nonfiction read-aloud selection for upper-elementary or middle-school students.

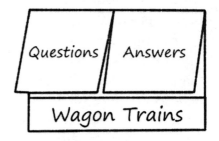

1 Ask your students if they have ever traveled more than 1,000 miles and how long the trip took. If they went on an airplane, it probably only took a few hours. Tell them that back in the 1800s, people traveled in covered wagons and it took many weeks to go 1,000 miles. Show some of the illustrations in the book and explain that a typical wagon was only 10 feet by 4 feet in size!

2 Measure off a 10' x 4' rectangle on the floor and have them imagine traveling thousands of miles in a covered wagon of that size.

3 Have each student create a two-flap graphic organizer and list at least five questions under the left flap (**Questions**) about how people traveled west in covered wagons.

4 Read the book aloud, stopping regularly so students can record their answers under the right flap (**Answers**).

Directions — Two-Part Flappers

From the Pattern:

1 Duplicate the pattern on page 56 or download the printer-friendly version at **www.lauracandler.com/gofr**.

2 Orient the page in the "portrait" direction as shown.

3 Fold the top part down to meet the solid horizontal line near the bottom edge of the paper.

4 Use scissors to cut on the solid line stopping at the fold, to create two flaps.

5 Write in the topic at the bottom edge of the flapper.

6 Write the category titles on top of each flap.

7 To use the flapper for taking notes or recording details, lift up the flaps and write the information underneath.

From Blank Paper:

1 Fold a blank sheet of paper in half lengthwise and open it up.

2 Orient the page in the "portrait" direction.

3 Use a ruler to draw a horizontal line about one inch from the bottom edge. Write your main topic under the line.

4 Fold the top part down to meet the line.

5 Use scissors to cut the top flap in half, creating two smaller flaps. Write the category titles on top of each flap.

6 Open the flaps and draw a line on the fold to divide the inside area into two sections.

7 To use the flapper for taking notes or recording details, lift up the flaps and write the information underneath.

Long Flappers

After students master the two-part flapper, you can introduce a slight variation—the long folded graphic organizer with three or four flaps. These long flappers can be turned either horizontally with the flaps opening upwards or vertically with the flaps opening sideways. The directions below feature a three-part flapper, but the same directions will work when creating one with four flaps.

Sample Lesson: Literary Connections

Teaching students to make connections while reading is an effective way to help them improve comprehension. This graphic organizer helps students make three types of connections:

TEXT TO SELF ● How can you connect this text to something you have experienced yourself?

TEXT TO TEXT ● How can you connect this text to another you have read? Have you read something similar or another book by this author?

TEXT TO WORLD ● How can you connect the events in this text to something in the real world?

The printable on page 60 is a pattern for a three-flap foldable, and the flaps include the types of connections and the guiding questions. You can duplicate the page or download a printer-friendly version of the Literary Connections flapper at **www.lauracandler.com/ gofr**. The first time you use this, introduce it to the whole class over the period of several days. Read aloud a realistic fiction chapter book like *Jake Drake, Bully Buster*, and stop every few pages to discuss and record connections.

Sample Lesson: Discussion Flappers

Literature circles are a great way to engage students in discussing books, but if students don't prepare for their meetings, those discussions can fall flat. One solution is to have each student create a Discussion Flapper (page 64) before the meeting. Then during the meeting, they can take turns sharing what they've written. Discussion Flappers can also be completed in literacy centers and used as preparation for a guided reading group discussion. You can duplicate the pages or download printer-friendly versions of the Informational Text Discussion Flapper and Literature Discussion Flapper at **www.lauracandler.com/gofr**.

Common Core Connections for Folded Flappers

RI 2.8, RI 4.8 – To describe how reasons support specific points the author makes in a text, write the specific points on the outside of each flap and record supporting details under each flap.

RL 4.3 – To describe a setting in a story or drama in depth, create a 2-part flapper. On the top of the left flap write *Time* and on the right flap write *Place*. Draw illustrations on the flaps that show how you visualize the setting. Under each flap write details from the text that provide clues and information about the setting.

RL 5.4 – Create a folded flapper with four or five flaps. On the outside of each flap, write a word or phrase from the reading selection. Write the meaning of the word or phrase under each flap.

RL 6.5 – Create a flapper based on one literary text to analyze how a particular sentence, chapter, scene, or stanza fits into the overall structure and contributes to the development of the theme, setting, or plot. On the outside of each flap, write a sentence, chapter title, or stanza. Under each flap, write details that explain the importance of that part to the whole selection. Consider how removing or changing that part might impact the overall story, how it serves as foreshadowing for future events, why the author chose to include that part, etc.

RL 2.10, RL 3.10, RL 4.10, RL 5.10, RL 6.10, RI 2.10, RI 3.10, RI 4.10, RI 5.10, RI 6.10 – The last standard for each grade level for both Informational Text and Literature states that by the end of the year, students should read and comprehend in their grade band proficiently with scaffolding as needed at the high end of the range. To meet this standard, you can use a variety of folded flappers throughout the year that include standard-specific flaps.

LAURA'S Tips

For additional topic suggestions for folded flappers, refer to the suggestions for T-charts and multi-column charts. Those graphic organizers can easily be converted into flappers with the number of flaps corresponding to the number of columns.

Directions — Three- and Four-Part Flappers

From a Pattern:

1 Duplicate the patterns on page 60 or 62, or download printer-friendly versions at **www.lauracandler.com/gofr**.

2 Fold the paper in half lengthwise.

3 Cut the top flap on the solid lines stopping at the fold, to create equal flaps.

4 Open the flaps and draw a vertical line below each cut to divide the inside area into three sections.

5 Write the category titles on top of each flap.

6 When taking notes or recording details, lift up the flaps and write the information underneath.

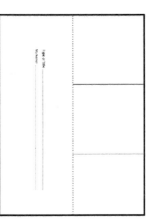

From Blank Paper:

1 To make a flapper with three parts, fold a blank sheet of paper into three equal parts as you would fold a letter. Then fold it in half lengthwise. (To make a flapper with four parts, fold your paper into four sections and then continue with the directions as shown below for three parts.)

2 Open the paper flat to see all the fold lines.

3 Fold paper in half lengthwise. Cut the top fold lines down to the middle of the page to create equal flaps.

4 Open the flaps and draw a vertical line below each cut, on the fold lines, to divide the inside area into three sections. Write the category titles on top of each flap.

5 When taking notes or recording details, lift up the flaps and write the information underneath.

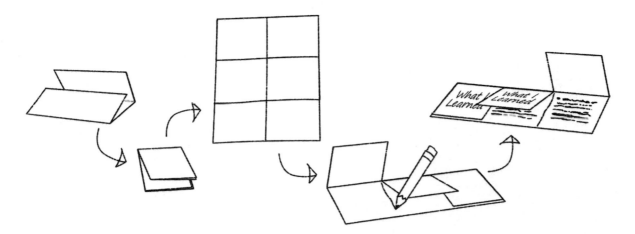

Topic or Title: _____

My Name: _____

LITERARY CONNECTIONS

My Name: _____

Text: _____

TEXT TO WORLD

How can you connect the events in this text to something in the real world?

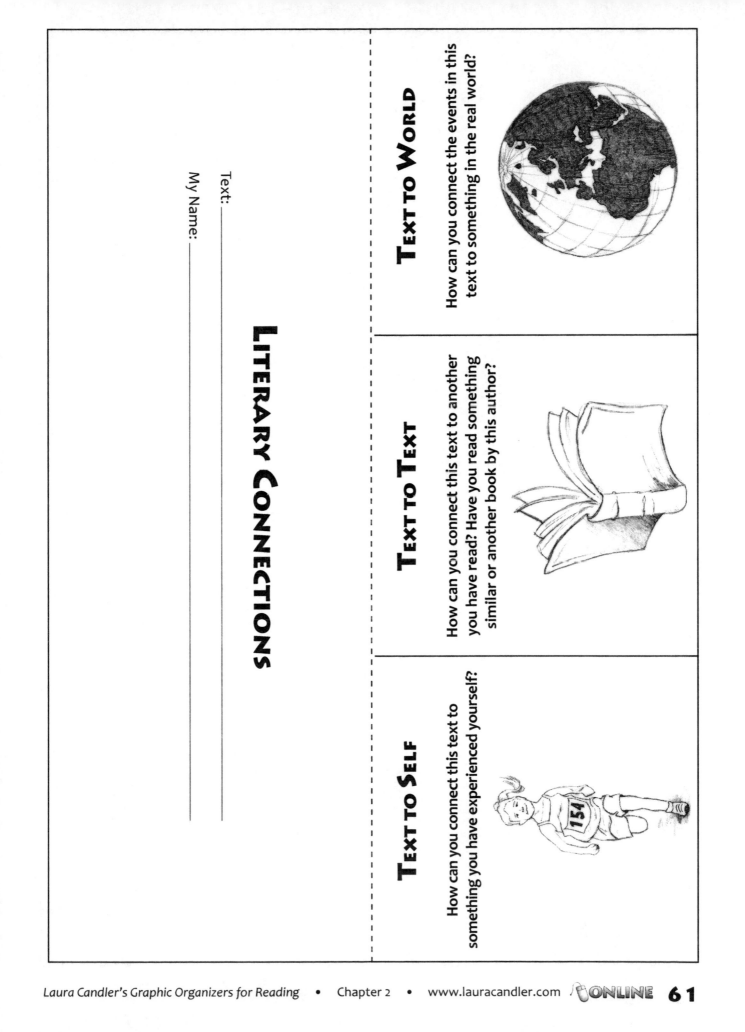

TEXT TO TEXT

How can you connect this text to another you have read? Have you read something similar or another book by this author?

TEXT TO SELF

How can you connect this text to something you have experienced yourself?

Title: _____

My Name: _____

INFORMATIONAL TEXT DISCUSSION FLAPPER

My Name: _____

Title: _____

MY REFLECTIONS

What surprised you? What do you think is the most important thing you learned? How can you use this information in your life? Would you recommend this book?

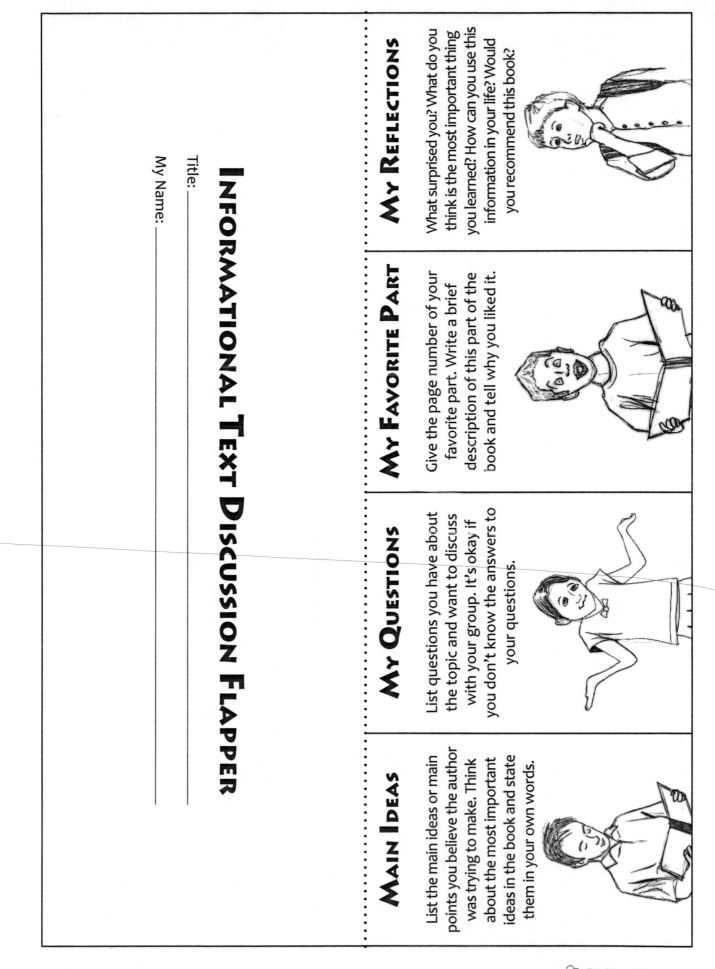

MY FAVORITE PART

Give the page number of your favorite part. Write a brief description of this part of the book and tell why you liked it.

MY QUESTIONS

List questions you have about the topic and want to discuss with your group. It's okay if you don't know the answers to your questions.

MAIN IDEAS

List the main ideas or main points you believe the author was trying to make. Think about the most important ideas in the book and state them in your own words.

Literature Discussion Flapper

My Name: _____

Title: _____

My Reflections

What do you think about the story so far? Can you make any predictions? What connections can you make to your own life or something you've read?

My Favorite Part

Give the page number of your favorite part. Write a brief description of this part of the book and tell why you liked it.

My Questions

List questions you have about the topic and want to discuss with your group. It's okay if you don't know the answers to your questions.

My Summary

Briefly describe what happened in this part of the selection. Include only the most important events and details.

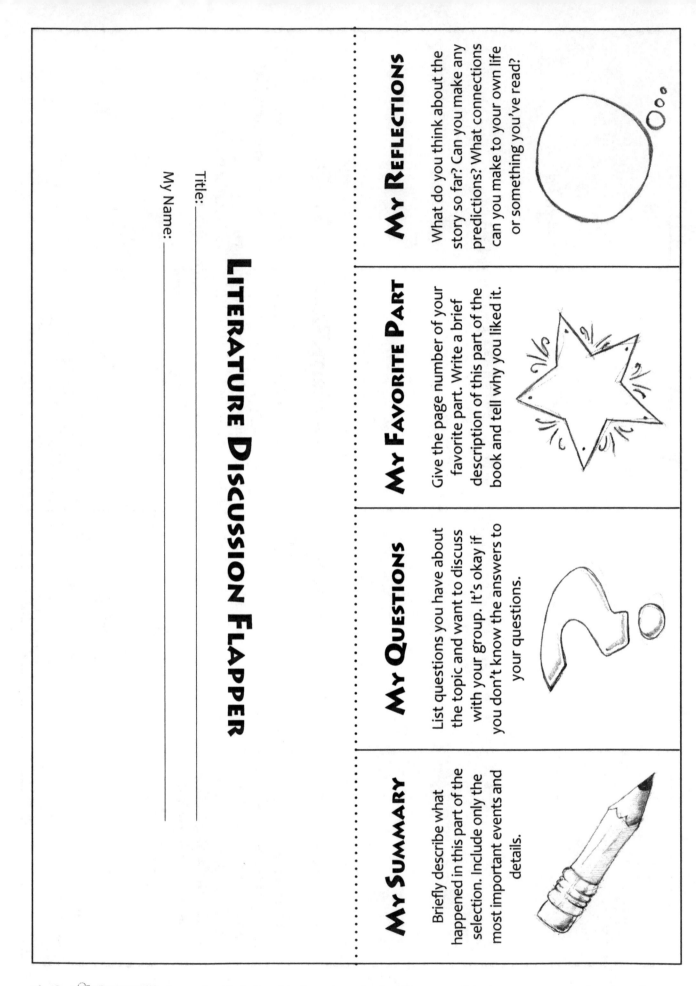

Sequencing Strips and Frames

Sequencing Frames

Sequencing frames are a series of boxes and arrows that are used to record the steps in a process or the order of events. Sequencing frames are very adaptable and easy to use because students aren't required to fill up a set number of boxes on a prepared worksheet. Instead, they begin by drawing a box in the top left corner of a blank page and adding frames and arrows across the paper, adding rows as needed.

Purposes

● Identify and record the steps in a process

● Show a sequence of events

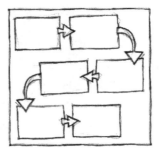

Sequencing Strips

Sequencing strips are the folded variation of Sequencing Frames. You can use the printable on page 68 the first time you do the activity, and later your students can cut, fold, and tape strips of paper without a pattern.

Fun Introduction:
All About Me

Students create a four-part timeline showing four important events in their own lives.

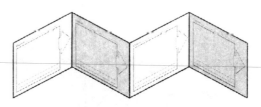

1 Duplicate the blank pattern on page 68 for each student or download the printer-friendly version at **www.lauracandler.com/gofr**.

2 Students cut the page horizontally in half on the dotted line across the middle to form two long strips. Then they fold each strip in half. They place the edges of the long strips together without overlapping them, and fasten with a small piece of clear tape.

3 In each of the four sections, ask each student to draw a picture of an important event in his or her life. Events could include their birth, the first day of school, a special vacation, etc. For each event, have them write an approximate date and a short descriptive title or caption.

4 After students finish their sequencing strips, give them time to share their work with their team or a partner.

5 To store the foldable, fold it accordion-style to create a small packet. Each student should write his or her name on the blank side of the front flap.

Sample Lesson: Main Event

After students are comfortable creating and using sequencing frames and sequencing strips, you can have them apply the concept to a story they are currently reading or one that you are reading aloud. Use the pattern on page 68 or download the printer-friendly version at **www.lauracandler.com/gofr**.

1 Have students begin by cutting, folding, and taping the graphic organizer as described in the Fun Introduction on page 65.

2 Then have them fold it into a packet and write the title and author of the book on the front. Be sure to have them flip their graphic organizers over and write their own names on the backs.

3 As students read or listen to the book, they complete the inside by sketching an illustration of a main event in the story on each section. Students should write a short caption below each picture to describe the main event they have illustrated. Each page provides room for four events in the book, so be sure to have extras on hand for students who are reading long books. An example based on a student's work is shown below.

4 Before you begin a new read-aloud book, have students create the strips and save them in a safe place. As you read the book on subsequent days, have them complete one frame each day. Discuss the main idea together as a class and ask them to write a one-sentence summary and sketch a picture of the main event.

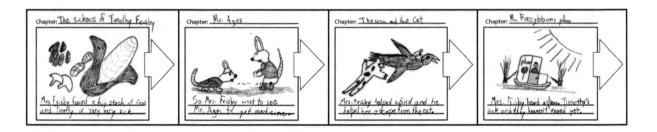

Common Core Connections

RL 2.7 – To demonstrate understanding of plot, use information gained from the illustrations and words in a print or digital text to create a plot sequence strip.

RI 2.3, RI 3.3 – Create sequencing frames or a sequencing strip based on a series of historical events, the steps in a technical procedure, or a scientific concept as it was developed over time. Use the sequencing frames as a reference when writing or discussing the connections between those events or steps. Use language that pertains to time, sequence, and cause/effect.

RL 3.2 – Use the events in a story, fable, folktale, or myth to create a plot sequencing strip. Determine the central message, lesson, or moral and refer to the sequencing strip as you explain how it is conveyed through key details in the text.

RI 3.8 – Create a series of sequencing frames using key sentences and paragraphs from a text. Use the sequencing frames as a reference when writing or discussing the logical connections (e.g., comparison, cause and effect, first/second/third in a sequence).

RI 4.3 – Create sequencing frames or a sequencing strip based on a series of historical events, the steps in a technical procedure, or a scientific concept as it was developed over time. Use the sequencing frames as a reference when explaining what happened and why, based on specific information in the text.

RL 6.3 – Create two sequencing strips and place one above the other as shown to describe how a particular story's or drama's plot unfolds in a series of episodes as well as how the characters respond or change as the plot moves toward a resolution. Record key events in the story's plot in the top strip, and write details about how the characters change and respond in the frames below each event.

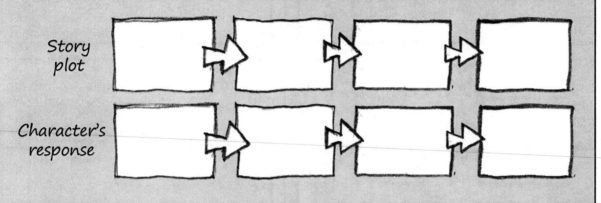

RI 6.3 – To analyze how a key individual, event, or idea is developed in a text, create a series of sequencing frames that show how a single character, event, or idea is introduced, illustrated, and elaborated.

RL 6.6 – Create a series of sequencing frames to explain how an author develops the point of view of the narrator or speaker in a text.

RI 6.6 – Determine an author's point of view or purpose in a text, and create a series of sequencing frames to explain how it is conveyed in the text.

RI 6.8 – Create a series of sequencing frames to trace and evaluate the argument and specific claims made in a text. Outline each frame in either blue or red to distinguish between claims that are supported by reason (blue) and claims that are not (red). In the blue boxes, briefly summarize the reasons and evidence that support those claims.

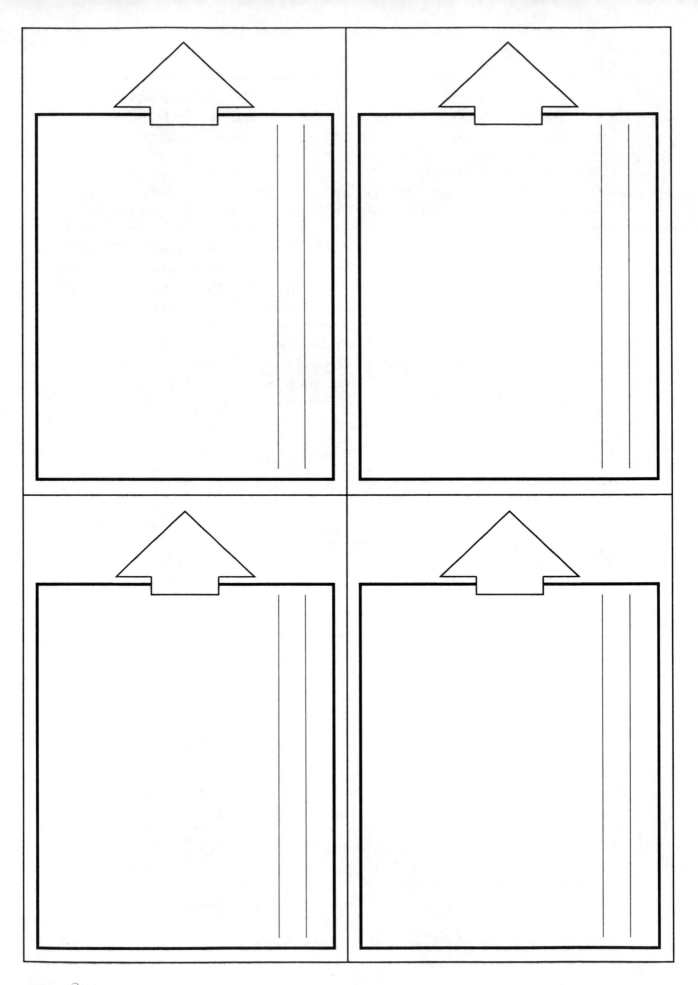

Sharing Boards

Sharing boards allow students to present information in a creative way. They can be used with both informational text and literature and they can easily be customized to include elements specific to the Common Core Standards for your grade level.

Purpose

● Take notes or record responses to literature for the purpose of sharing them with others

Fun Introduction:
Friendship Sharing Boards

1 To begin this activity, assign partners who don't know each other well but who are likely to work comfortably together. Give each student a blank copy of the Sharing Board on page 71 or a large piece of white drawing paper. If they use drawing paper, they'll need to fold it into eighths and draw bold lines on the folds to separate the blocks.

FRIENDSHIP SHARING BOARD			
NAME	**FAMILY**	**SPECIAL PLACE**	**FAVORITE BOOK/AUTHOR**
HOBBIES & INTERESTS	**CONNECTIONS**	**SPECIAL QUALITIES**	**FUTURE PLANS**

2 Display the directions shown on page 72.

3 Ask students to take turns interviewing each other about the categories on the board and completing the sections. Give them a set time for working on each block—I suggest no more than five minutes per block. Tell students that stick figures and simple drawings are fine.

4 After the students complete their boards, create groups of four students by combining two sets of pairs. Give them time to introduce their partner to the others in the group and to briefly share the most important elements on their boards.

Sample Lesson: Informational Text and Literature Sharing Boards

After students understand how to create Sharing Boards, they will be able to use them to display information about books they're reading. The Literature Sharing Board is a little easier for students, so you might want to begin with that one.

1 Have each student fold a large sheet of construction paper into eighths and display the directions (page 73 or 74).

2 Explain exactly what you expect students to do in each section. The first time you use the Sharing Board, you may want have them complete each section, one at a time, after you explain the directions. It will probably take several days for them to complete the graphic organizer the first time you introduce it. Before they begin working, clearly set forth your expectations for the quality of their work. If you want detailed drawings, complete sentences, and correct spelling, be sure students are aware of those expectations before they begin.

3 As students are completing their graphic organizers, monitor their work to be sure they are meeting the standards you have set forth.

4 The blank Sharing Board pattern on page 71 is provided if you would like to create your own set of directions.

Common Core Connections

RL 2.10, RL 3.10, RL 4.10, RL 5.10, RL 6.10, RI 2.10, RI 3.10, RI 4.10, RI 5.10, RI 6.10 – The most advanced Literature Standard for each grade level states that by the end of the year, students should read and comprehend literature in their grade band proficiently with scaffolding as needed at the high end of the range. In the same way, the most advanced Informational Text Standard states students should read and comprehend informational texts proficiently, including history, social studies, science, and technical texts. To meet these Standards, you can customize the blank sharing board on page 71 by adding different labels and directions to each section. If you use the sharing board graphic organizer with different types of informational and literary texts throughout the year, your students will develop reading proficiency over time.

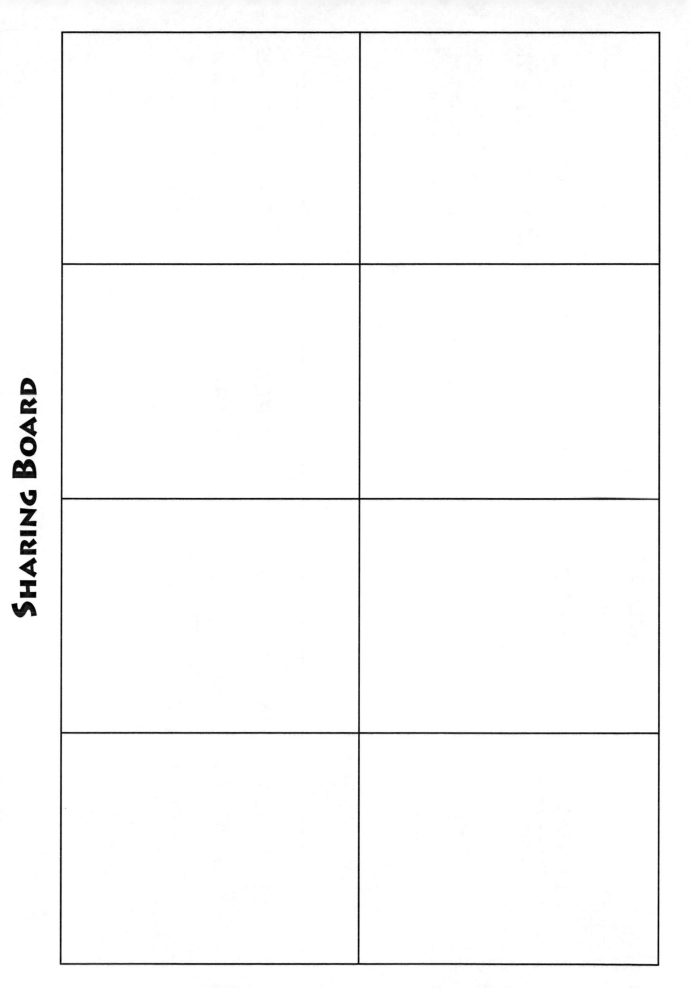

SHARING BOARD

Friendship Sharing Board

Name write your friend's name here in bold letters Sharing Board created by Your Name	**Family** Draw and/or write about your friend's family, including any pets.	**Special Place** Draw and/or write about your friend's favorite vacation spot or special place to visit.	**Favorite Book/Author** Write the title and author of your friend's favorite book or author.
Hobbies & Interests What does your friend enjoy doing in his or her spare time? Draw or write about it!	**Connections** What connections do you have with this friend? Draw and/or write about how you are alike.	**Special Qualities** List at least 3 of your friend's special qualities. Draw a picture or symbol to represent one or more of them.	**Future Plans** Draw and/or write about what your friend hopes to do or to be when he or she grows up.

Informational Text Sharing Board

Write the key words at the top of the block. Then complete the block according the to directions below.

Title **Author**	**Main Idea**	**Chart, Graph or Illustration**	**Vocabulary**
Sharing Board by Your Name	What is the main idea of the book? Write a sentence that gives the main idea in a simple yet complete statement.	Create a chart, graph, or other illustration to display some of the information you learned in the book.	List and define or illustrate at least 3 important vocabulary words from the book.
Amazing Fact	**Connections**	**Beyond the Text**	**Evaluation**
Draw a picture and write a caption to share an amazing fact that you learned from the book.	How can you connect this information to something in your life or something you have read? Illustrate or explain in words.	Where do you think you could look for more information on this topic? Draw a picture and/or write a sentence to explain.	Write a few sentences that describe how you felt about the book. You may also use pictures or symbols.

LITERATURE SHARING BOARD

Write the key word for each section at the top of the block.
Then complete the block according to the directions below.

TITLE	SETTING	CHARACTERS	BEGINNING
AUTHOR Sharing Board by Your Name	Draw a picture and write a caption to describe the time and location in which the story took place.	Draw a picture of the main characters and label your illustration.	Draw a picture and write a caption to describe the events at the beginning of the story.
MIDDLE Draw a picture and write a caption to describe the events in the middle of the story.	**CLIMAX** Draw a picture and write a caption to describe the story's climax (high point of action).	**CONCLUSION** Draw a picture and write a caption to describe the conclusion (ending).	**EVALUATION** Write a few sentences that tell how you felt about the story. You may also use pictures or symbols.

Attribute Charts

An attribute chart consists of a matrix of columns and rows that can be used to compare the features of related texts. Many of the more complex Common Core Standards can be taught with attribute charts that compare and contrast literary elements across texts from different authors, different cultures, or different sources. Because these charts are more complex and often require students to reference multiple texts, they frequently require more than one day to complete.

Fun Introduction:
Compare attributes of students in your classroom

On chart paper or a white board, create a blank chart with at least three columns and four rows. Write headings such as **Name**, **Hair Color**, and **Favorite Book** at the top of each column. Including one physical attribute and one non-physical attribute will demonstrate that attributes don't have to be tangible. Ask student volunteers to come forward, one at a time, to write their names in the left column and the appropriate details in the other columns. Then ask interpretive questions from the chart such as, "Who has brown hair?" or "Whose favorite book is *Stone Fox*?"

Purposes

- Organize concepts according to their attributes

- Compare and contrast features and information in related texts

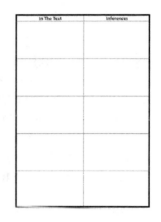

In The Text	Inferences

Students in Mrs. Smith's Class		
Name	Hair Color	Favorite Book
William	brown	Redwall
Javier	black	Maniac Magee
Thomas	blonde	Stone Fox

Sample Lesson: Comparing Fiction Genres

Students frequently have difficulty distinguishing the various fiction book genres. An attribute chart can help them see relationships between different types of literature.

1 Use the chart on page 79 or create your own chart with genres your class will be studying. The example on page 80 shows how to complete a genre chart focused entirely on fiction. Genre charts should be completed over a period of days or even weeks so students don't become confused and overwhelmed.

2 Before you introduce each genre and add it to the chart, gather an assortment of books to use as examples in the lesson.

3 Show the books to the class and explain the characteristics of that genre.

4 Have students record the details across the row next to the genre title and brainstorm other examples. Students should keep these charts in a reading log or folder as a reference.

5 In addition to the Fiction Genre Chart, you may want to do one for various types of informational texts or one that helps them distinguish between types of folklore such as myths, legends, fairy tales, and fables.

Common Core Connections

RL 2.4 – Create a two-column attribute chart to describe how words and phrases (e.g., regular beats, alliteration, rhymes, repeated lines) supply rhythm and meaning in a story, poem, or song. Title the left column **Words and Phrases** and the right column **Rhythm and Meaning**. In the left column list words and phrases from one story, song or poem. In the right column, write information about how those phrases add to the rhythm and meaning in the story, song, or poem.

RL 3. 4, RL 4.4 – To determine the meaning of words and phrases as they are used in a text, create a three-column attribute chart. From left to right, label the columns **Words and Phrases, Literal Meanings**, and **Nonliteral Meanings**. For each word written in the left column, write a definition in the second column, and figurative or connotative meanings in the third column.

RL 3.6 – To help distinguish between various points of view in literary selections, create a four-column attribute chart. Use the column labels from left to right: *Selection Title, Author's Point of View, Character's Point of View, My Point of View*. As you read each selection, write in the title and use clues to determine and record each point of view.

RL 3.9 – Use a four-column attribute chart to compare and contrast the themes, settings, and plots of stories written by the same author about the same or similar characters (e.g., in books from a series). Label the columns from left to right: *Title, Setting, Plot, Theme*. Read several selections by one author about the same characters and record the details for each book in one row.

RL 4.5 – Use a three-column attribute chart to explain major differences between poems, drama, and prose, and to refer to the structural elements of poems and drama. Title the far left column *Genre* and label the boxes below the title with the words, *Poetry, Prose*, and *Drama*. Title the next column, *Examples*, and the far right column, *Structural Elements*. After reading several examples of poetry, prose, and plays, list examples of each in the second column and distinguishing structural characteristics like verse, rhythm, stanzas, paragraphs, casts of characters, dialogue, scripts, etc.

RL 4.6 – Create a two-column attribute chart to compare and contrast the point of view from which different stories are narrated, including the difference between first- and third-person narrations. Label the columns *Story Title* and *Narrator's Point of View*. As you read each story, record the title on the left and details about the narrator's point of view on the right.

RL 4.9 – To compare and contrast the treatment a similar topic in literature from different cultures, create a three-column attribute chart. Choose one topic to explore and locate stories from different cultures that deal with that topic. In the far left column, list the story titles. Title the next column *Culture* and list information relevant to each culture. Title the far right column *Treatment of Topic* and include information about story elements like character traits, setting, and plot, as well as similarities and differences in how the stories treat the topic.

RL 5.5 – Create a two-column attribute chart based on one literary text to analyze how a particular sentence, chapter, scene, or stanza fits together to provide the overall structure of a particular story, drama, or poem. Label the left column *Selection from Text* and the right column *Importance to Overall Structure*. In the left column, write a sentence, chapter title, or stanza. In the right column, write details that explain the importance of that part to the whole selection. Consider how removing or changing that part might impact the overall story, how it serves as foreshadowing for future events, why the author chose to include that part, etc.

RL 5.6 – To describe how a narrator's or speaker's point of view influences how events are described, create a two-column attribute chart with headings *Actual Events* and *Narrator's Description*. In the first column, write specific events that happened in the story and describe them in objective or factual terms. In the second column, write details about the narrator's description of that same event, and notate how the narrator's point of view may have impacted the way the event was described.

RL 5.9 – To compare and contrast stories in the same genre on their approaches to similar topics, create an attribute chart based on texts from one genre. Locate several stories from that genre that deal with similar topics, and list the story titles in the far left column. Label the other columns with story elements like *Characters, Setting, Plot*, and *Theme*. As you read each text, complete the corresponding row by writing details in the columns.

RL 6.1 – To cite textual evidence to support analysis of what the text says explicitly as well as inferences drawn from the text, create an attribute chart for one text that has two columns. Label the left column *In the Text* and the right column *Inferences Drawn from Text*. In the left column, list specific details from the text. In the box to the right of each detail, write inferences that can be drawn from what was stated in the text.

RL 6.4 – Create a four-column attribute chart based on one text to help determine the meanings of words and phrases used in the text and to analyze the impact of specific word choice on meaning and tone. From left to right, label the columns *Words and Phrases, Literal Meanings, Nonliteral Meanings, Impact*. For each word or phrase or written in the left column, write a definition in the second column, the figurative or connotative meanings in the third column, and the impact on meaning and tone in the fourth column.

RL 6.5 – Create a three-column attribute chart to analyze how a particular sentence fits into the overall structure and contributes to the development of the theme, setting, or plot. From left to right, title the columns *Sentence, What the Sentence Means, How It Relates to the Text*. When considering how the sentence relates to the text, imagine how the story would be different if you removed the sentence, how it provides clues about future events, what we can infer from the sentence, why the author chose to include it, etc.

RL 6.9 – To compare and contrast texts in different genres in terms of their approaches to similar topics, create a three-column attribute chart on one topic or theme. Label the columns from left to right with these headings: *Text, Genre, Treatment of Theme/Topic*. As you read a variety of texts on this topic, record the text title, its genre, and details regarding how the text approaches that particular topic.

COMPARING FICTION GENRES

Genre	Characters	Settings	Plot Elements	Examples
Realistic Fiction				
Historical Fiction				
Science Fiction				
Fantasy				
Mystery				

Comparing Fiction Genres

Genre	Characters	Settings	Plot Elements	Examples
Realistic Fiction	real or made-up people and/or animals that behave in normal ways	• real places • present times	events that could really happen and that an average person might experience	• Holes • The Great Gilly Hopkins
Historical Fiction	real or made-up people and/or animals that behave in normal ways	• real places • past times	events that could have happened to the character and historical events that did happen	• Boston Jane: An Adventure • Number the Stars
Science Fiction	real or imaginary people and/or creatures	• any location in the universe • generally present or future times	events that seem unlikely but could happen as a result of future technology	• The City of Ember • The Time Hackers
Fantasy	real or imaginary people and/or creatures that often have special abilities	• any location, real or imaginary • any time period	often based on magic, witchcraft, or super powers; animals may behave as humans	• The Lightning Thief • Ella Enchanted
Mystery	real or imaginary people and/or creatures of any type	• any location, real or imaginary • any time period	clues are given in the beginning and middle of a story; mystery is solved near the end	• The Boxcar Children • Cam Jansen series

CHAPTER 3

Graphic Organizers for Informational Text and Literature

Graphic Organizers
for **Informational Text** and **Literature**

● ● ● ● ● ● ● ● ●

The 23 graphic organizers in this chapter have specific uses for informational text and literature. The first five can be used for informational text. The next eight graphic organizers work well with both informational text and literature. The last ten apply to literature.

I've included the following information for each graphic organizer:

● Common Core Standards met by using the organizer

● Whether the organizer is for informational text, literature, or both

● Targeted reading strategies

● Suggested texts that work well with the graphic organizer

● General description and overview

● Step-by-step techniques for teaching the graphic organizer

If your students have never used a particular graphic organizer, it's best to introduce it to your whole class first. Then have students work with a partner to complete one after reading a selection together. Finally, assign the graphic organizer for independent practice. Refer to Chapter 1 for more detailed information on the "I Do, We Do, You Do" technique for introducing graphic organizers to your class (p. 14). Spending a minimum of several days on each graphic organizer will ensure that your students understand how to use the graphic organizer, as well as learn the reading strategy and meet the Common Core Standard. All the suggested texts in this chapter are listed in the Bibliography of Suggested Texts on page 152.

The following list shows all the graphic organizers in this chapter, and indicates whether they are appropriate for informational text, literature, or both.

Informational Text

- Informational Text Features Search
- Informational Text Structures
- Main Idea Neighborhood
- Biographical Bits
- Research and Record

Both

- On Target Questions
- KWL and KWLS Charts
- News Hound Summary
- Vocabulary Flapper
- Cause and Effect Rockets
- It All Adds Up
- Seeing Is Believing

Literature

- Character Trait Map
- Stick Figure Character Map
- Character Feelings Flow Map
- Summarizing Sequencer
- Story Map Variations
- Step-by-Step Predictions
- Literary Response Scroll
- Poetry Peace Map
- Poetic Reflections

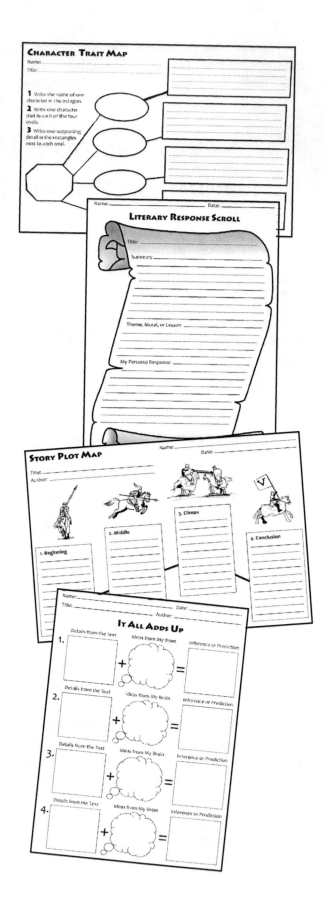

Informational Text Features Search

Common Core Standards:
RI 2.5, RI 3.5

Reading Strategies

- Identify text features within informational texts

- Deepen understanding of how various text features aid in reading comprehension

Suggested Texts

Gravity: Forces and Motion

National Geographic Kids Ultimate Dinopedia: The Most Complete Dinosaur Reference Ever

Informational texts are organized differently from literary texts in order to make the information easier to read and understand. Theses selections often include "features" such as subheadings, maps, sidebars, diagrams, captions, and illustrations to help convey the meaning of the text clearly. Digital text often includes hypertext and other interactive elements. The Informational Text Features Search serves as a place to record those features, and it also helps students identify the author's purpose for using them. This graphic organizer will help your students explore how text features help their reading comprehension.

Step by Step:

1 Choose one selection from a basal text, news article, or nonfiction book that has a variety of informational text features. Give each student a copy of the graphic organizer on page 88. Ask your students to help you search for the informational text features in the selection.

2 As you record those features on the class chart, have students record them on their own charts.

3 Ask your students how each feature helps them comprehend the text by imagining what the text would look like without that feature. Sample questions include:

- Does an image help you visualize the way something looks?

- Does a diagram or chart help you understand a process?

- Do boldfaced words help you identify key vocabulary?

4 Repeat with additional informational text selections.

Title: _____ Date: _____

INFORMATIONAL TEXT FEATURES SEARCH

Title:		
Page #	Text Feature	How It Helps Comprehension

Title:		
Page #	Text Feature	How It Helps Comprehension

bibliography	glossary	Internet link	subheading
bold print	graph	italic print	table of contents
bullet points	heading	map	timeline
caption	illustration	photograph	use of color
diagram	index	sidebar	website interactive element

Informational Text Structures

Common Core Standards:
RI 3.8, RI 4.5, RI 5.5, RI 6.5

Reading Strategies

● Identify the overall text structure of an informational selection

● Recognize that some informational selections may include more than one text structure

Suggested Texts

Multiple informational texts

Text structures are different from text features, and students often confuse the two. "Features" are contained within the text, and "structures" refer to how the entire selection is organized. Informational texts may be organized in many ways. Some are in chronological order, but more commonly they're presented in chunks like main topics and subtopics, questions and answers, problems and solutions, or causes and effects. Luckily, each type of structure is characterized by certain clues within the text (refer to page 92 for examples of clue words). A long selection may contain several different organizational structures within the full text.

Due to the complexity of this topic, you may want to spread this instruction out over several weeks and introduce just one or two new text structures per week.

Step by Step:

1 Give each student a copy of the blank chart on page 91 to store in his or her reading log.

2 Introduce each text structure using a text that is a clear example of that structure. Have students look for clue words that might help identify the structure and add those to the chart. Refer to the sample chart on page 92 for the types of clues that go with each text structure. In the column on the far right, ask students to write the title of the text you used as your example. They should write small and leave room to add at least one more title.

3 Later in the week, try to share at least one more example of a text that's organized in the same way, and ask students to try to find their own examples as they read. Then ask students to list one or two examples for that text structure. The examples may be news articles, short nonfiction books, or selections from their basal reader.

4 After you have introduced the major text structures, ask students to begin analyzing the text structures of any nonfiction selections they read.

LAURA'S Tips

Good sources of informational text include print and online news magazines, basal readers, content-area textbooks, newspaper articles, editorials, and short nonfiction books.

INFORMATIONAL TEXT STRUCTURES

Structure	Clues	Examples
Description or List		
Cause and Effect		
Compare and Contrast		
Problem and Solution		
Chronological or Sequential Order		
Question and Answer		
Topics and Subtopics		
Other		

INFORMATIONAL TEXT STRUCTURE CLUES

Structure	Clues	Examples
Description or List	adjectives, descriptive language, lack of action, lists of attributes or characteristics	
Cause and Effect	reasons, results, causes, because, reason why, effect, affect	
Compare and Contrast	similar, like, different, differences, however, but, another, both	
Problem and Solution	problem, difficulty, answer, solution	
Chronological or Sequential Order	times, dates, first, next, last, then, after that, before	
Question and Answer	who, what, where, when, why, how, wonder, question marks	
Topics and Subtopics	long text divided into sections with separate headings, bold and regular fonts	
Other		

Main Idea Neighborhood

Reading Strategies

- Find the topic and main idea of a text
- Recount the key details and explain how they support the main idea

Suggested Texts

Martin's Big Words

The Important Book

Distinguishing between the main idea and its supporting details is a necessary informational text comprehension skill. This graphic organizer helps students clarify their understanding of these terms by comparing them to a neighborhood (topic), streets (main idea), and houses (details).

Step by Step:

1 The Main Idea Neighborhood graphic organizer is best introduced with a paragraph or short informational text selection that has one clear topic, a main idea, and a few supporting details.

2 Give each student a copy of the graphic organizer (p. 94) and read your chosen selection aloud.

3 Explain that the topic is a word or short phrase that states what the selection is about, and ask them to help you name the topic.

4 To find the main idea, they should ask what the selection is telling about that topic and express it in a sentence. The main idea might be a sentence they can copy directly from the text or they might create it on their own. For example, the topic might be "Pet Care," and a main idea sentence might be, "Caring for a pet requires time and effort."

5 Have them look for supporting details such as, "Many dogs need to be taken outside for exercise several times a day."

6 Share the neighborhood analogy by asking them to imagine a neighborhood with streets and homes. If the neighborhood is the topic, each street is a main idea, and the houses on each street represent the details.

7 Extend the lesson by analyzing a multi-paragraph selection that has one topic for the entire selection and a different set of main ideas and details for each paragraph.

Main Idea Neighborhood

Name: _____

Title: _____

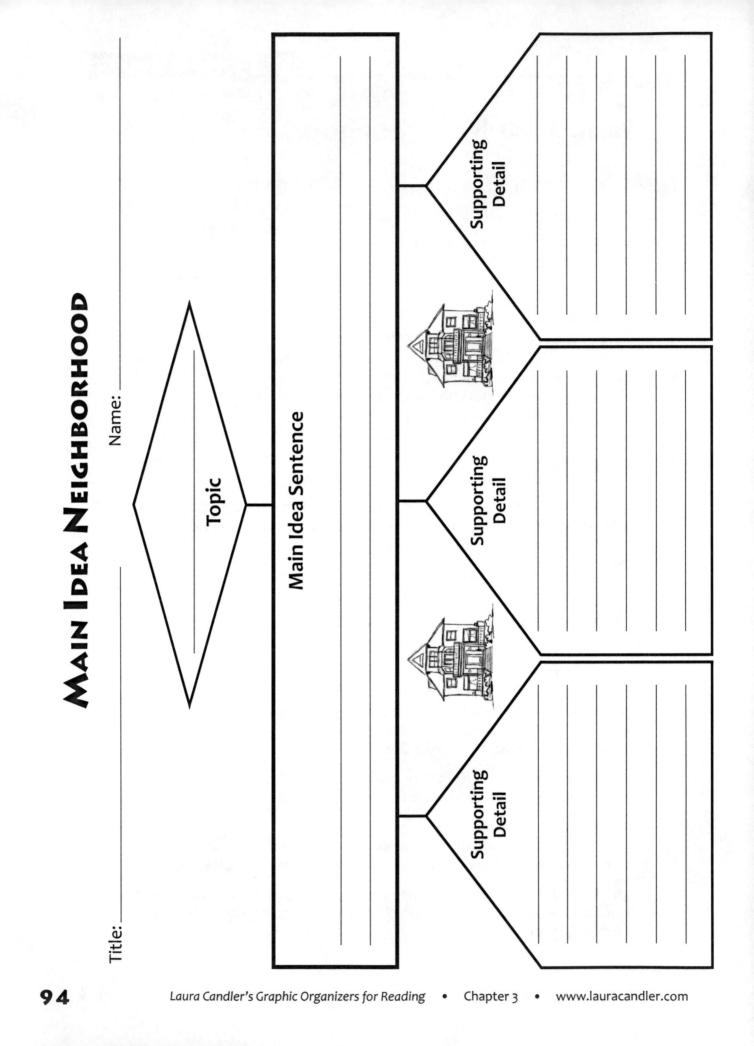

Topic

Main Idea Sentence

Supporting Detail

Supporting Detail

Supporting Detail

Biographical Bits

Reading Strategies

- Comprehend biographical texts
- Identify and classify important details
- Conduct research using multiple sources

Suggested Texts

Who Was Dr. Seuss?

Jackie Robinson: Strong Inside and Out

Students are often expected to research a famous person prior to writing a report, but frequently their notes are nothing more than sentences copied from the source. Biographical Bits requires students to think about what's most important and classify the information into categories. Because space is limited, they learn to take notes using bulleted lists and simple phrases. I've included three variations of the form on the following pages; the third variation (page 98) is blank so you can add your own headings.

Step by Step:

1 Choose one of the three Biographical Bits graphic organizers, read aloud a short biography, and ask students to jot down important details on individual dry-erase boards or in journals.

2 Then call on one student at a time to share a detail and tell where they think it belongs on the graphic organizer. After all the notes are recorded, have a student draw or paste a picture of the person in the center.

3 To give students more experience with reading biographical texts, ask them to use at least two sources of information for this research activity. The graphic organizer on page 97 includes a place for them to list their sources in whatever format you require. If they are using a different graphic organizer, they can list their sources on the back.

4 You can extend this research activity by having your students use their notes as the basis for writing a short essay about the famous person. If they write one paragraph for each category, it should be easy for them to write a well-organized essay.

BIOGRAPHICAL BITS

Name: _____

Date: _____

Subject of Biography: _____

Early Life

_____
_____
_____
_____
_____
_____
_____
_____
_____
_____

Adult Life

_____
_____
_____
_____
_____
_____
_____
_____
_____
_____
_____

Accomplishments

_____
_____
_____
_____
_____
_____
_____
_____
_____

Impact on Society

_____
_____
_____
_____
_____
_____
_____
_____
_____
_____

BIOGRAPHICAL BITS

Name:_____

Date:_____

Subject of Biography:_____

Personal Life

_____
_____
_____
_____
_____
_____
_____
_____
_____
_____
_____
_____

Accomplishments

_____
_____
_____
_____
_____
_____
_____
_____
_____
_____

Impact on Society

_____
_____
_____
_____
_____
_____
_____
_____
_____
_____
_____

Information Sources

_____
_____
_____
_____
_____
_____
_____
_____
_____
_____
_____

BIOGRAPHICAL BITS

Name: _____

Date: _____

Subject of Biography: _____

Research and Record

Reading Strategies

- Read and comprehend informational texts
- Conduct research using multiple texts and types of sources
- Integrate information obtained from multiple texts and sources

Suggested Texts

Multiple texts on a single topic in both print and digital formats

The Research and Record graphic organizer is a two-page form to use when researching a specific topic and recording information from multiple sources. Many grade levels include a Common Core Standard about integrating information from several texts and sources on the same topic in order to write or speak about the subject knowledgeably. To help students meet this Standard, the second page of the graphic organizer includes a list of possible information sources as well as a place to list the actual sources used. The Research and Record graphic organizer is also useful when teaching students how to narrow the research topic. Because there are only three sections for taking notes, students will need to identify three subtopics within the main topic and record their notes in the appropriate sections. This space limitation requires your students to use bulleted or abbreviated note-taking form rather than copying entire sentences and paragraphs from their sources. After students complete the research and note-taking process, they can integrate the information to write an essay or speech on that topic.

Step by Step:

1 Introduce the graphic organizer a day or two before you assign a research project for students to complete independently. For your demonstration lesson, choose a topic that's similar to the types of topics you will be assigning. For this example, if your students will be expected to research an invention, select the light bulb as the topic of your introductory research lesson. Before starting to teach the lesson, locate several different types of digital and print sources of information on that topic.

2 Display both pages of the Research and Record graphic organizer (pages 102 and 103) and tell students that they will be using this form to take notes when researching their own topics. Tell them that you want to share some tips for using the form to take notes.

3 Write **Invention of the Light Bulb** at the top of the first page and then ask them to think about the kinds of information they might find when researching this topic. Brainstorm a list of ideas on the board, such as: inventor, year invented, how it was invented, how it works, how the invention has changed over time, how it has impacted people's lives, the future of the invention, etc. Then explain that there's so much information available on this topic that they need to focus on just three subtopics. For the purposes of this lesson, we'll use **How Invented, Changes Over Time**, and **Impact on Our Lives**.

4 Demonstrate how to write each of the three subtopics at top of the note-taking sections.

5 Point out the list of possible sources on the second page. Ask your students which sources they would consult when looking up information about the invention of the light bulb. They should think about the three subtopics they have selected when considering their sources. For example, a book, article, or website might give information about how the light bulb was invented or changed over time, but they may want to conduct interviews to find out how it has impacted our lives. Point out that the area below the list of sources is where they will record the title of each source and/or the name of the person they interview.

6 Use a document camera or projector to display one of the digital or print sources of information you found prior to the lesson. Locate a section of text that has relevant information and read it aloud. Ask students to raise their hands when they hear something that should be added to the graphic organizer. Show them how to write the information from the text in their own words in bulleted note form rather than copying the entire sentence or paragraph. Continue to model the note-taking process using several more selections. To actively engage your students, have them use individual dry-erase boards to practice writing notes in bulleted or abbreviated form.

7 After your students practice writing notes from one selection, turn to the back of the graphic organizer and show them how to record that source on the lines under *Information Sources*. The format you use will depend on your students' grade level and your expectations for them. Some teachers may find a list of titles to be sufficient, while others may prefer a more traditional bibliographic format.

8 To fully meet the Common Core Standards for research, your students will need to use the information in the graphic organizer as the basis for writing a short essay or speech on the given topic. If they write one paragraph for each category, it should be easy for them to write a well-organized essay that integrates information from multiple sources.

LAURA'S Tips

If you want to know which notes came from each source, have students color-code their notes and sources. For example, put a blue dot next to each note obtained from a book, a green dot next to notes taken from an article, etc. They would put a corresponding color-coded dot next to each title in their bibliography.

Name:

Research and Record

Topic:

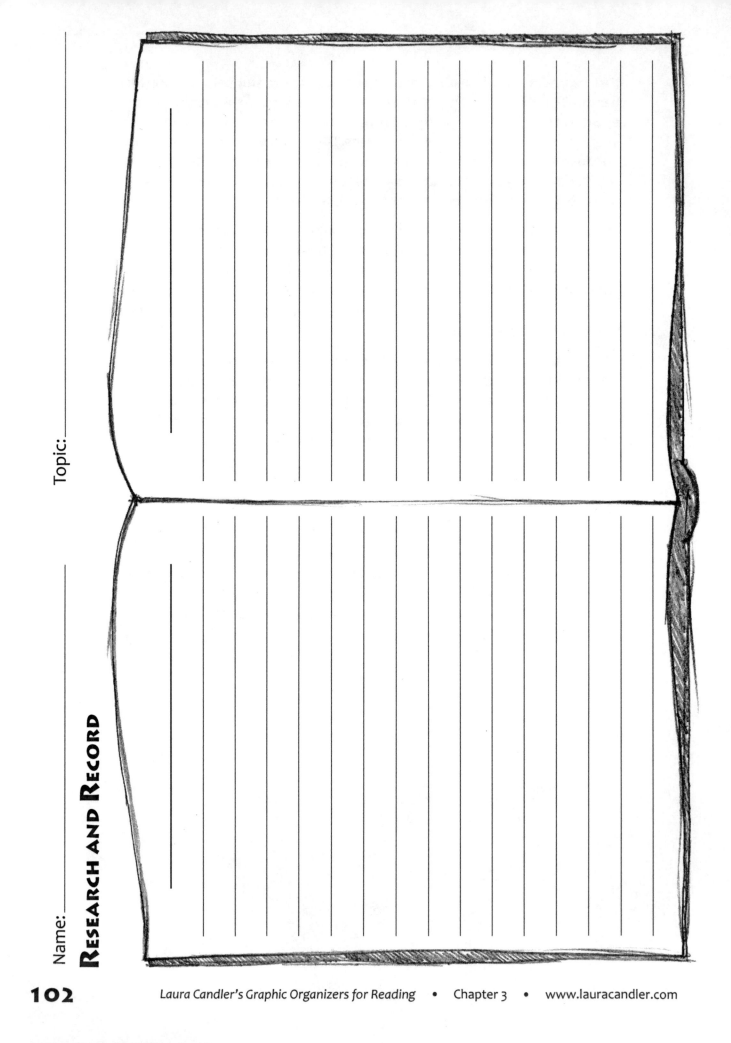

Laura Candler's Graphic Organizers for Reading • Chapter 3 • www.lauracandler.com

Name: _____

RESEARCH AND RECORD

Information Sources

Circle each type of source you used and record the titles of those sources on the lines below.

book   encyclopedia   website   article   video   survey

interview   atlas   documentary   other

On Target Questions

Common Core Standards:
Informational: **RI 3.1, RI 3.7, RI 5.7**
Literature: **RL 3.1**

Reading Strategies

● Ask and answer questions to demonstrate understanding of a text, referring explicitly to the text as the basis for the answers

Suggested Texts

The Best Book of Volcanoes

Eyewonder: Weather

The On Target Questions graphic organizer is designed to help students practice asking and answering questions while reading. Learning to ask specific questions is an important critical thinking skill that is often overlooked in reading instruction. Being able to ask the right questions allows the reader to dig deeply into the text, look for details, and extract the full meaning of the selection. When introducing this graphic organizer, locate articles and texts that are organized with headings and subheadings. With those types of reading selections, it's often easy to turn the subheadings into questions. For example, if an article about snakes has a subheading of "Helpful Critters," you might ask, "How are snakes helpful critters?"

Step by Step:

1 Start by giving each student the same article and practicing together as a class. Choose a text that includes clear headings and subheadings. Ask them to write the name of the article in the middle of the "target" on the graphic organizer (p. 106).

2 Ask students to skim through the article to see how the text is organized and to think of questions that could probably be answered from the selection.

3 Have the students write one question in each of the four sections inside the middle oval. Discuss their choices as a class and allow all students to use the same four questions.

4 As they read, ask them to look for the answers and jot them down in the outer sections of the target using bulleted lists or short phrases.

LAURA'S Tips

Creating questions from subheadings is a challenging task for many students. You may want to repeat the whole class lesson several times with different texts before students are ready to work with a partner or on their own.

On Target Questions

Title: _____

Date: _____

Write the selection title in the middle. Use the sub-headings to write four questions in the inner ring. Then read the selection and write the answers to the questions in the outer ring.

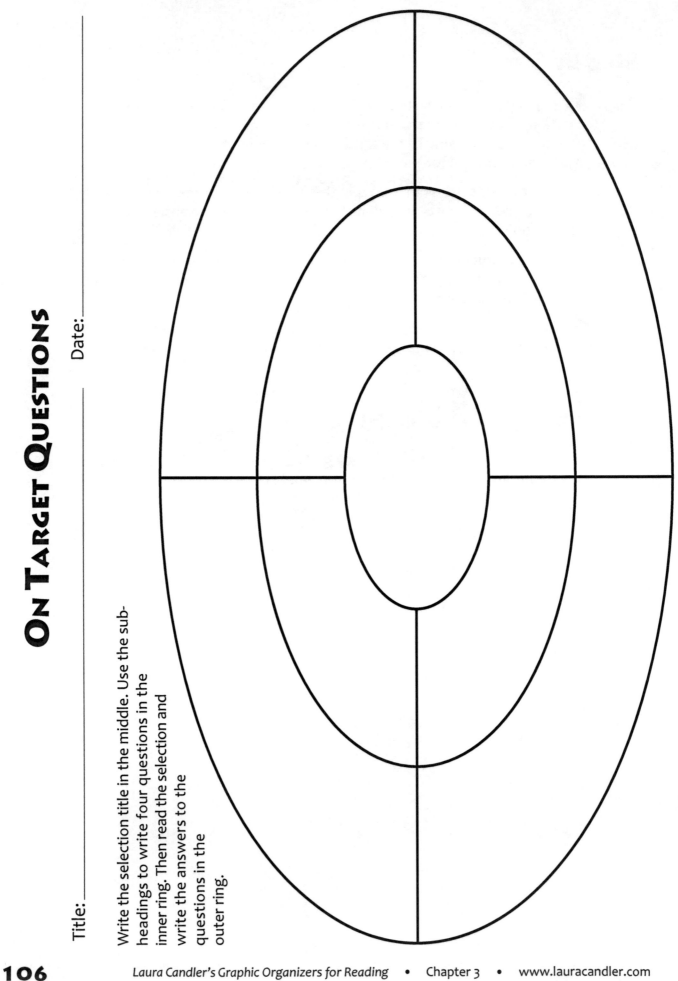

KWL and KWLS Charts

Reading Strategies

- Examine prior knowledge before reading
- Ask questions to set purposes for reading
- Read nonfiction texts for understanding
- Record facts and details
- Determine where to search for more information

The KWL (Know-Wonder-Learned) Chart was explained in Chapter 1, but the graphic organizer is included here because it works with both informational texts and literature. Use it before reading a story that requires knowledge of a particular scientific or historical concept. For example, before reading a historical fiction book, have the class complete a collaborative KWL chart based on the particular time period in which the story is set. The four-column KWLS (Know-Wonder-Learned-Search) Chart is a variation of the KWL chart. When students are reading informational texts, they are often interested in learning more. The "Search" column prompts students to list the places where they can search for more information.

Suggested Texts

The Wagon Train

Nature's Green Umbrella: Tropical Rain Forests

Step by Step (KWLS Chart):

1 Introduce the KWL chart as described on page 18 before introducing the KWLS Chart.

2 After students are familiar with the KWL chart, read aloud a short selection that references a topic that students might want to explore further.

3 After you complete the "L" column with what they learned, add the fourth column and ask them where they could search for more information. For example, they might search on the Internet, in a particular magazine, or in other nonfiction books on related topics. They might also interview an expert or plan to visit a local museum.

KWL Chart

Name: _____

Date: _____

Title or Topic: _____

Know	Wonder	Learned
Before you read, write what you think you know about the topic.	Before or as you read, write what you wonder or want to know about the topic.	While reading or after you finish, take notes about what you learned.

KWLS Chart

Name: _____

Date: _____

Title or Topic: _____

Know	Wonder	Learned	Search
Before you read, write what you think you know about the topic.	Before or as you read, write what you wonder or want to know about the topic.	While reading or after you finish, take notes about what you learned.	After you finish reading, where can you search for more info on this topic?

News Hound Summary

Reading Strategies

- Identify the facts and details in a news article
- Summarize important facts in a informational text selection

Suggested Texts

The Mary Celeste: An Unsolved Mystery from History

Magic Tree House Fact Tracker #7: Titanic: A Nonfiction Companion

Learning to write a concise summary that includes only the relevant details is a difficult skill for most students. The News Hound Summary makes the process easier by providing a place for students to first list the details, and then use those facts to write a short summary. Students can find appropriate articles in the local newspaper, in print magazines like *Scholastic News* or *Time for Kids*, or online at websites like ScienceNewsforKids.org. The News Hound Summary can also be used with literary texts; ask students to pretend they are news reporters trying to find all the important facts about what happened in the reading selection.

Step by Step:

1 Model the News Hound Summary in a whole-group setting with class participation. Give each student a blank copy of the organizer (p. 111) and a copy of the same news article or story.

2 Ask them to read the article carefully and become "news hounds," looking for *who, what, when, where, why,* and *how* the events happened. They should highlight those details and then share them with the class as you fill in the chart together.

3 Demonstrate how to use that information to write a brief summary of the most important events in the article. As they write, they can imagine themselves as reporters writing a news report about the main events in the story.

4 You may have to model this skill several times in a whole-group or small-group setting before your students will be ready to complete it on their own.

News Hound Summary

Name:_____

Selection Title:_____

Question	Facts from the Selection
Who?	
What?	
Where?	
When?	
Why?	
How?	

Super Sleuth Summary

Use the facts you uncovered and listed above to write a one-paragraph summary of the selection.

_____

_____

_____

_____

_____

_____

_____

_____

_____

_____

_____

Vocabulary Flapper

Reading Strategies

- Understand vocabulary needed to comprehend informational text

- Generate symbols and write sentences for topic-specific vocabulary

Suggested Texts

Sweet Clara and the Freedom Quilt

Sylvester and the Magic Pebble

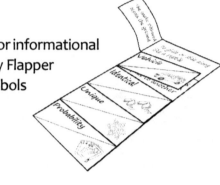

Learning new vocabulary before reading a story, poem, or informational text will help students with comprehension. The Vocabulary Flapper assists in this process by having students create visual symbols for new words, in addition to using them in sentences.

Step by Step:

1 The first time your students create a Vocabulary Flapper, give them the template on page 114. You can also download a printer-friendly version at **www.lauracandler.com/gofr**. After your students know what to do, all they need is a plain sheet of paper. Have students fold their papers in half length-wise and cut down to the fold four times to form five flaps.

2 Choose five vocabulary words from the selection they will be reading, and ask them to write one word on the outside of each flap in the top triangle.

3 Use a variety of strategies to teach the words to your students. You can assign each team one word to look up and teach to the class, or you can teach the words yourself. Give examples of definitions and how to use each word in a sentence.

4 After you have introduced each word, give students time to complete the other three sections related to that word. In the bottom triangle of the top flap, under the word, have students draw a symbol or picture that will help them remember the word. Then have them open the flap and write the definition and a sentence.

5 When all the flaps are completed, allow time for students to share their pictures and sentences with their team or with the class.

Vocabulary Flapper Example

Inside of Flapper
Sentences and Definitions

To glide or slide along like a reptile	The snake slithered across the ground.
Something that takes people or goods from one place to another	Five vehicles drove by in two minutes.
Exactly alike and equal	Are those two girls identical twins?
Being the only one of its kind	Every snowflake is different and unique.
A number express-ing the likelihood of an event; chance	The meteorologist said the probability of rain is 30% today.

Outside of Flapper
Words and Symbols

Slither

Vehicle

Identical

Unique

Probability

Vocabulary Flapper

Name: _____

Date: _____

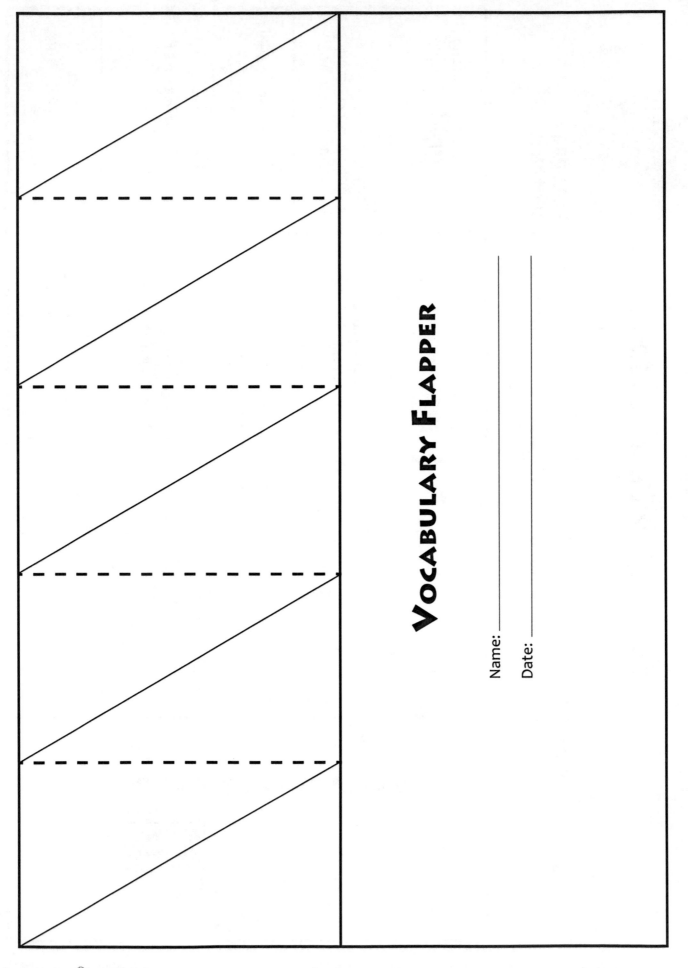

Vocabulary Flapper

Name: _____

Date: _____

Cause and Effect Rockets

Common Core Standards:
Informational: **RI 2.3, RI 3.3, RI 3.8, RI 5.3**
Literature: **RL 2.3, RL 3.3**

Reading Strategies

- Identify cause and effect relationships
- Recognize that a single event may have multiple causes and effects

Suggested Texts

The Teacher from the Black Lagoon

Nothing Ever Happens on 90th Street

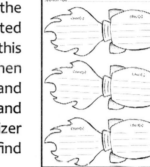

When we name two events, how can we tell the cause from the effect? We know that the cause comes first and the effect is the result of what happened. However, sometimes the effect is stated in a selection before we find out its cause. One way to teach this concept is to ask your students to think about what happens when a rocket takes off. First, the fuel is ignited and begins burning, and then the rocket blasts off. Most narratives include many cause and effect relationships as the plot develops. This graphic organizer also works well with news articles where the reader can often find multiple causes and effects.

Step by Step:

1 The first time you introduce Cause and Effect Rockets, use a text that has at least three fairly clear cause and effect relationships. Read the text aloud and ask the students to help you find the cause and effect relationships as you record them.

2 Later, model how to use it with texts that include an event with one cause and many effects, or one effect and many causes.

3 Use this graphic organizer on a regular basis to give students an opportunity to explore the complexity of cause and effect relationships.

LAURA'S Tips

Sometimes an effect becomes the cause of another event taking place, so it's fine for students to rewrite the effect from one rocket in the flame of the next rocket. Also, remember that causes and effects aren't always one-to-one relationships; sometimes a single cause will have multiple effects or a single effect may have multiple causes.

CAUSE AND EFFECT ROCKETS

Name: _____

Date: _____

Selection Title: _____

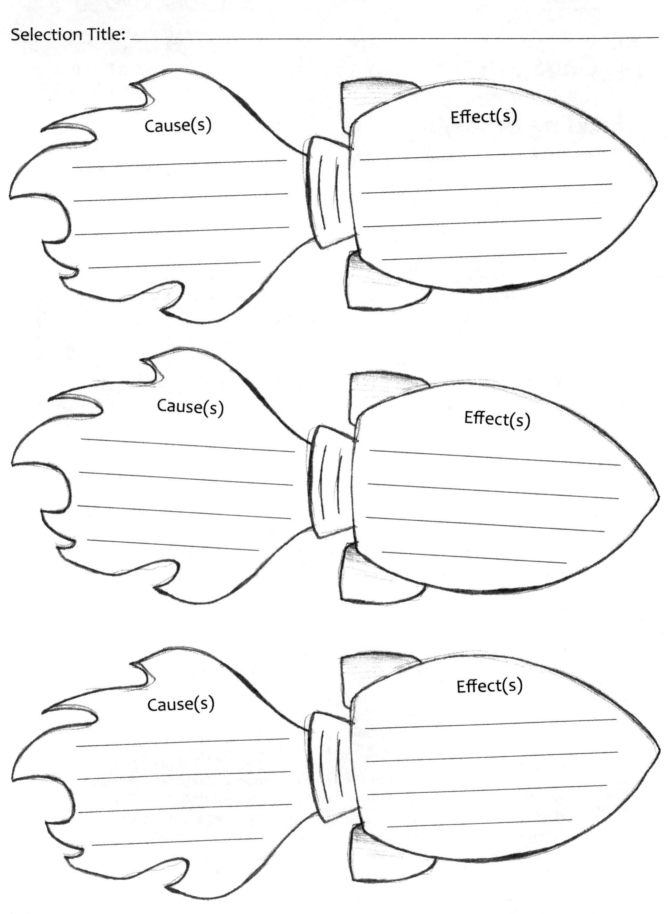

Cause(s)

Effect(s)

Cause(s)

Effect(s)

Cause(s)

Effect(s)

It All Adds Up

Reading Strategies

- Inferring and predicting by using details from the story paired with prior knowledge

- Understanding the difference between inferences and predictions

Suggested Texts

Crickwing

The Wretched Stone

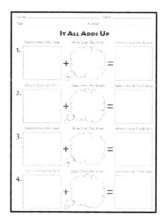

The strategies of inferring and predicting are often confusing to students. Both of them involve noticing important details in a selection and adding information that you already know to "read between the lines," or figure out something that is not directly stated in the text. The difference between them is that inferring involves events that have already happened or are currently taking place, and predicting is making an informed guess about what you think will happen in the future. It All Adds Up can be used when teaching students about inferences alone, predictions alone, or both concepts together. The lesson below is specifically designed for teaching the difference between inferring and predicting; refer to the T-chart Common Core Connections on page 40 for suggestions about how to teach each skill independently.

Step by Step:

1 Read a short selection that includes opportunities to infer and predict.

2 Stop reading at the first point where the reader needs to make an inference in order to understand what's happening.

3 Ask students to talk with a partner about what they think is taking place in the story and then share their ideas with the class.

4 Display a copy of It All Adds Up (p. 119) and explain that they were able to understand what was happening because they noticed important details in the story and added information from their brains to infer meaning.

5 Show them how to complete the sections of the graphic organizer and record the actual inference on the far right. Circle the word "Inference" above the inference statement.

6 Read a little more and stop where students can easily make a prediction. Explain the difference between inferring and predicting and ask them to make a prediction about what will happen next. Record the details and ideas as well as a prediction statement. Circle the word "Prediction" above the prediction.

7 As you continue reading, stop in two more places and ask students to make an inference or a prediction and record their details and prior knowledge accordingly.

8 Later, students should practice this graphic organizer again with a partner or in a learning center.

LAURA'S Tips

When using It All Adds Up with informational text, the "answer" to each equation will almost always be an inference rather than a prediction. However, analyzing news articles may result in predictions; students may want to predict what will happen in the future based on the events in the article.

Name: _____ Date: _____

Title: _____

It All Adds Up

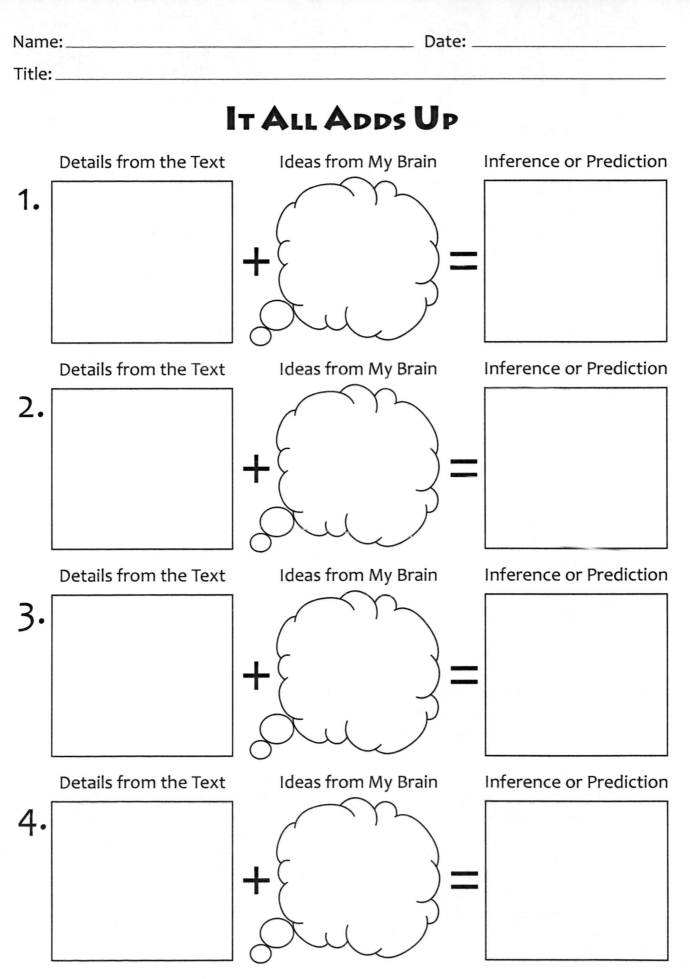

Details from the Text   Ideas from My Brain   Inference or Prediction

1.   +   =

Details from the Text   Ideas from My Brain   Inference or Prediction

2.   +   =

Details from the Text   Ideas from My Brain   Inference or Prediction

3.   +   =

Details from the Text   Ideas from My Brain   Inference or Prediction

4.   +   =

Seeing Is Believing

Common Core Standards:
Informational: **RI 2.7, RI 3.7, RI 4.7**
Literature: **RL 3.7, RL 5.7**

Reading Strategies

- Understand how images that accompany a text contribute to the meaning of that text

- Interpret information presented visually, orally, or quantitatively

Suggested Texts

Water Dance

The Magic School Bus and the Electric Field Trip

The advent of the computer age has transformed the way our students read. For thousands of years, the act of reading meant looking at black text on a static white page. Today, reading has evolved. Books often include visual elements, from fancy fonts to color photographs to intricate charts and diagrams. Information presented digitally may include sound, animation, and interactive elements. Because the way we read has changed, we need to adapt our reading instruction to address these changes. This new awareness is reflected in the Common Core Standards for both Informational Text and Literature. Most grade levels include at least one Standard regarding the sometimes complex interactions between a text and its visual elements.

Step by Step:

1 Prior to beginning the lesson, locate a variety of short texts or websites in which the visual or interactive elements contribute to or clarify the meaning of the text. Science websites that include animation work well for this lesson. Choose one or two of these selections to use in your demonstration lesson, and make the others available to students for independent work or partner practice.

2 Without showing the text or web page, read aloud a short selection that would be difficult to understand without seeing the accompanying illustrations or animations. Ask students if they found any part of what you read to be confusing. What questions come to mind that aren't answered by the words alone? What seems to be missing from the text? Ask students what they might do if they were the author and were trying to help the reader understand the text. Hopefully, they will suggest drawing a picture or making a chart to show the information in another way.

3 Show them the page or website you read from and reread the selection while they look at the visual elements. If a website includes animation, play the animation several times. What visual elements do they see on the page? How do the visual elements or animation help the reader gain a deeper understanding of the words on the page? In the case of literature, do the illustrations contribute to the mood, tone, or beauty of the story? Do they help emphasize important aspects of the characters or the setting?

4 Display a copy of the Seeing Is Believing graphic organizer (p. 122). Demonstrate how to describe one visual element in each box across the top row. Below each visual element, describe the effects of that element on the reader's understanding of the text. Keep your students actively engaged by having them complete each part of the graphic organizer on individual dry-erase boards as you walk them through the lesson.

5 Give each student a blank Seeing Is Believing graphic organizer to complete alone or with a partner. For younger students, provide an assortment of appropriate texts and online selections for students from which students can choose for this assignment. Older students can choose their own selections if they are taught to look for books and websites in which the visual elements are necessary for a complete understanding of the text.

LAURA'S Tips

Because this lesson requires students to examine visual elements on a page, it's almost essential to use a document camera to display a print text or a computer with a projector to display a website or e-book version of a text. If those technologies are not available, teach the lesson to small groups of students so they can gather around your book or computer.

SEEING IS BELIEVING

Name: _____

Date: _____

Title: _____

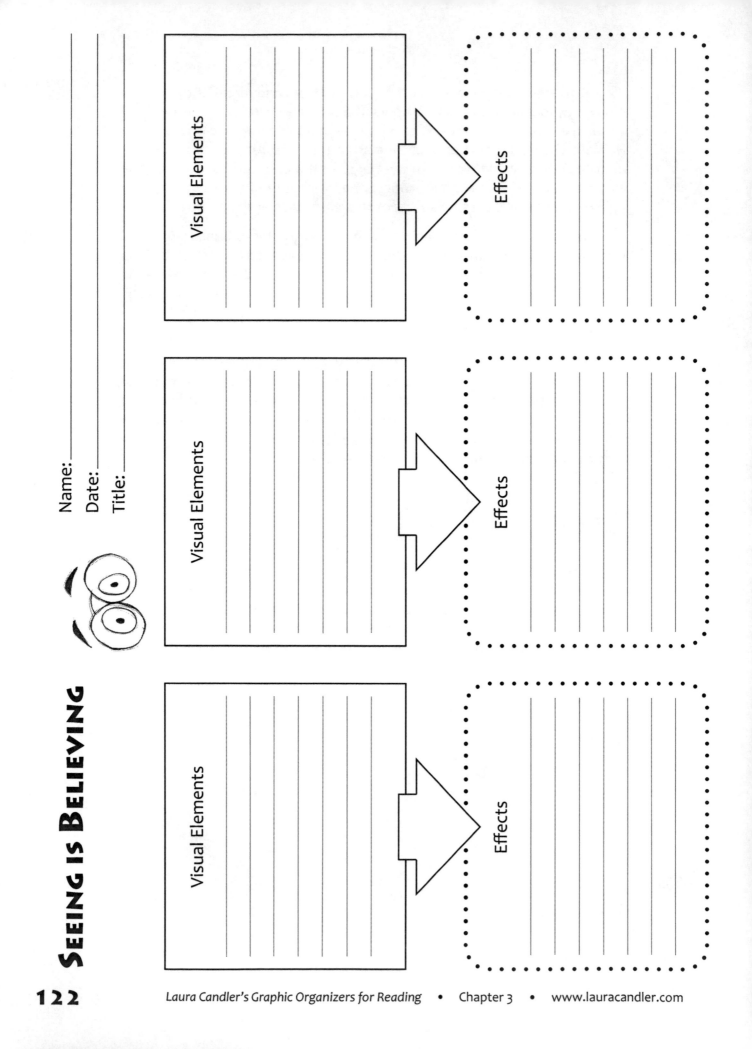

Visual Elements

Effects

Visual Elements

Effects

Visual Elements

Effects

Character Trait Map

Reading Strategies

- Identify character traits
- Justify responses with details from the text

Suggested Texts

Wilma Unlimited: How Wilma Rudolph Became the World's Fastest Woman

The Rough-Face Girl

Learning to infer character traits from story details is an important skill that develops over time. Authors generally do not state character traits explicitly in text; instead, they demonstrate those traits through the character's thoughts, words, and actions, as well as by what other characters say about them. Character trait terms often have layers of meaning that aren't conveyed through simple definitions, so it is critical that sufficient time be given to discuss nuances of meaning.

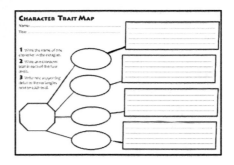

Step by Step:

1 Duplicate one copy of the two character trait lists (page 126 or 127) for each student and laminate it for students to keep as a reference.

2 Give each student a copy of a blank Character Trait Map (p. 125) to use during your whole-group lesson. Start by explaining that a "trait" is a word that describes the personal qualities of the character, and refer to their list for examples.

3 Read aloud a short book and ask your students to identify the main character's traits. Have each student write one trait and its supporting detail on an individual dry-erase board or scrap paper and hold it up for review. Select one trait to add to the chart and explain what that trait means, to be sure all students understand.

4 Ask your class to help you identify details from the story that support this character trait. After sufficient class discussion, each student should record the details on his or her own chart.

5 If this is a part of a mini-lesson, add just one or two traits to the chart on the first day and complete it the next day.

6 Later in the week, read another short text aloud and ask students to work with a partner to fill out another Character Trait Map. Collect their work and review it for accuracy.

7 By the end of the week, your students should be ready to complete a Character Trait Map on their own. Be sure to revisit this skill several times throughout the year with a wide variety of characters.

LAURA'S Tips

Developing an understanding of key character traits is a skill that takes time; as you teach this lesson, you'll discover many gaps in your students' understanding of these words. Rather than trying to finish the chart all at once, it's better to spend class time thoroughly discussing each trait and complete the chart over several days

CHARACTER TRAIT MAP

Name: _____

Title: _____

1 Write the name of one character in the octagon.

2 Write one character trait in each of the four ovals.

3 Write one supporting detail in the rectangles next to each oval.

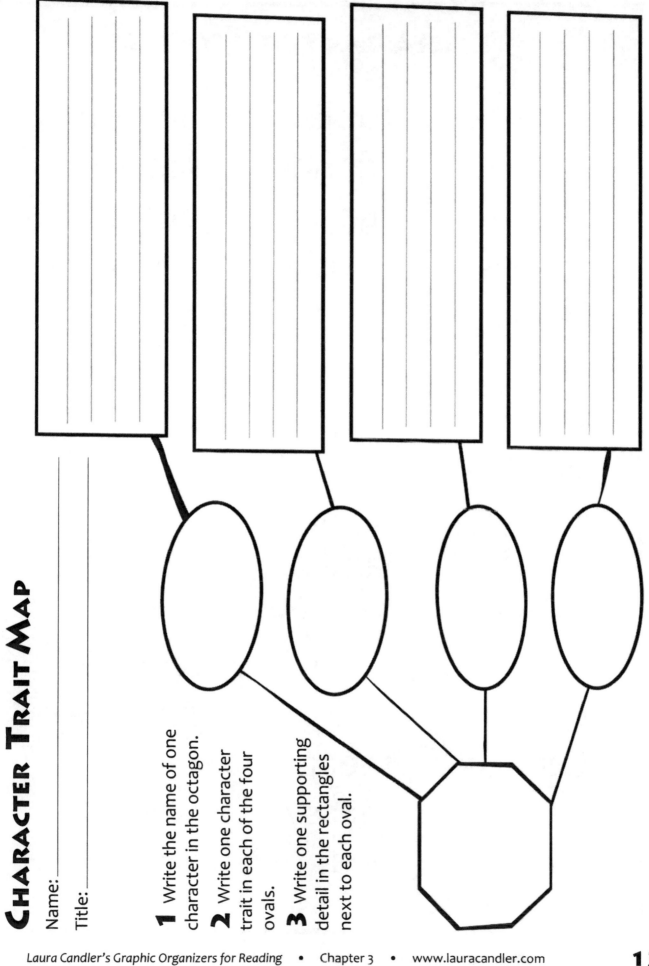

CHARACTER TRAITS

active	foolish	nervous
afraid	friendly	picky
angry	funny	polite
babyish	gentle	proud
bored	giving	quiet
bossy	grouchy	rude
brave	helpful	sad
busy	honest	selfish
calm	joyful	shy
careful	lazy	silly
caring	loving	smart
cheerful	loyal	sneaky
clumsy	lucky	stubborn
curious	mean	sweet
eager	messy	wild
fair	neat	wise

CHARACTER TRAITS

absent-minded
adventurous
ambitious
anxious
argumentative
bashful
bold
bossy
brave
careless
caring
cautious
cheerful
clever
clumsy
conceited
confident
considerate
content
courageous
cranky
creative
critical
cruel
curious
dainty
daring
dedicated
defiant
demanding
determined
devious
dishonest
disrespectful

dreamer
energetic
even-tempered
friendly
fun-loving
generous
gentle
greedy
gullible
handsome
happy
hard-working
helpful
heroic
honest
humble
humorous
imaginative
impatient
impulsive
independent
innocent
intelligent
inventive
joyful
lazy
leader
logical
lovable
loving
loyal
mannerly
messy
methodical

mischievous
obedient
open-minded
optimistic
outgoing
outspoken
patient
patriotic
persistent
pessimistic
polite
proud
reckless
resourceful
respectful
rude
selfish
serious
shy
sly
sneaky
spendthrift
spoiled
stingy
stubborn
studious
successful
suspicious
thoughtful
timid
unruly
unselfish
wasteful
witty

Stick Figure Character Map

Reading Strategies

● Create a visual image of a character based on details from the story

● Infer a character's thoughts and motives from his or her actions

Suggested Texts

The Pain and the Great One

Train to Somewhere

The Stick Figure Character Map gives students the opportunity to visualize what a character might look like and to bring the character to life by adding details to a stick figure outline. In order to complete the assignment, students also have to infer what the character might be thinking or feeling. Developing a deeper understanding of each character will help students comprehend the story and infer a character's motives. When evaluating student work, consider how well they followed the directions rather than their artistic ability.

Step by Step:

1 The week before you plan to do this activity, let the students know that they will be drawing a book character and adding details to represent the character's thoughts, feelings, and actions. Ask them to read a short book or story with an interesting character and bring it to class on the given day.

2 Prepare an example of a completed Stick Figure Character Map in advance. Model this activity with the class using a character in a well-known story or movie, or a character in a book your class has read together. You could also use the sample on page 131, which is based on the book *No More Dead Dogs*. If you are using a document camera to show your work, you'll need to switch back and forth between the directions on page 129 and your example. Read the directions aloud, show them your completed graphic organizer and explain why you chose to add each detail.

3 An alternative way to model the graphic organizer is to create the example while the students watch. Ask your students to provide details that you quickly sketch. Then post the directions and give them their own copy of the Stick Figure Character Map (p. 130) to complete.

STICK FIGURE CHARACTER MAP
DIRECTIONS

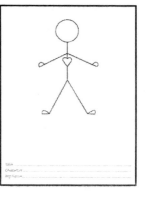

1 At the bottom of the page, write the selection title, the character's name and your name.

2 Add facial features, hair, clothing, and other details to show how the character might appear in real life.

3 Near each body part, neatly draw and color the details below:

● **Head**—Draw a thought bubble near the head and write what the character might be thinking.

● **Mouth**—Draw a speech bubble near the mouth and write what the character might say.

● **Heart**—Near the heart, draw a picture of something or someone the character loves, or write words to describe the character's feelings.

● **Hands**—Near one of the hands, draw something the character might hold or use.

● **Feet**—Near one of the feet, draw or write a sentence to describe where the character might have been or might like to go.

Title: _____

Character: _____

My Name: _____

Dreams or thoughts
Who is trying to reck the play?
"So I'm quitting team to go back and work on Old Shep, My Pal."
Actions
Playing football on his school team the giants
love
The play, (Old Shep My Pal)
Places
My character spends a lot of time in the gym during reheaple
Book Title No More Dead Dogs
Character Wallace Wallace
My Name Halle Auf Der Heide

Character Feelings Flow Map

Reading Strategies

- Identify characters' feelings and justify choices with details from the selection

- Observe how characters' feelings may change throughout a text

Suggested Texts

Enemy Pie

A Bad Case of Stripes

One reason many students love to read fiction is that they can identify with the characters' feelings. However, they may have difficulty verbalizing those feelings and seeing that the story's characters, like real people, often experience different feelings from one moment to the next. Use this graphic organizer with your class to foster rich discussions about these topics.

Step by Step:

1 Choose a short text in which the character's feelings change at least three times.

2 Distribute copies of the Character Feelings Flow Map (p. 133) to your students and show them that the graphic organizer has two separate flow maps for two different selections; you'll complete the first one together and they will do the second one with a partner or alone.

3 Ask them to look at the "feeling words" in the word bank at the bottom of the page. Explain the meanings of any unfamiliar words and share details from your own experience as examples.

4 Discuss the differences between feelings and traits: feelings can change from moment to moment, but character traits are more permanent and describe the overall qualities of the person. For example, someone may feel angry because of a particular event, but that doesn't mean he or she is an angry person.

5 Read the selection aloud and ask your students to help you identify how the character feels at the beginning, middle, and end of the story. Below each "feeling word," jot down the supporting details from the story.

6 Later, have students read another literature selection alone or with a partner and complete the second flow map on the page.

Name: _____ Date: _____

CHARACTER FEELINGS FLOW MAP

Title: _____ Character: _____

Beginning	**Middle**	**End**
Character's Feelings _____ Explanation or Details	Character's Feelings _____ Explanation or Details	Character's Feelings _____ Explanation or Details

Title: _____ Character: _____

Beginning	**Middle**	**End**
Character's Feelings _____ Explanation or Details	Character's Feelings _____ Explanation or Details	Character's Feelings _____ Explanation or Details

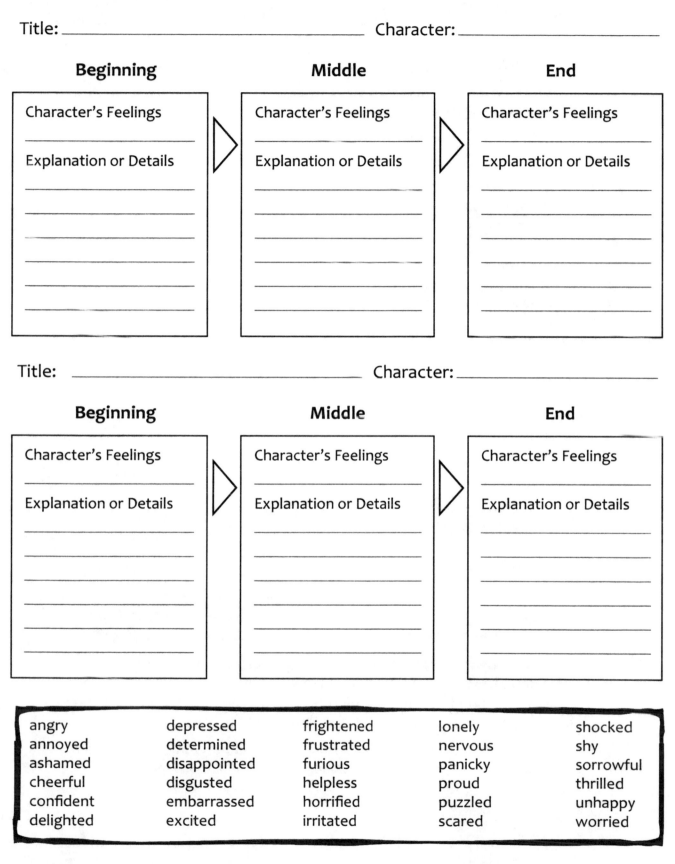

angry	depressed	frightened	lonely	shocked
annoyed	determined	frustrated	nervous	shy
ashamed	disappointed	furious	panicky	sorrowful
cheerful	disgusted	helpless	proud	thrilled
confident	embarrassed	horrified	puzzled	unhappy
delighted	excited	irritated	scared	worried

Summarizing Sequencer

Common Core Standards:
RL 2.5, RL 3.2, RL 4.2,
RL 5.2, RL 6.2

Reading Strategies

● Identify the main events in a literary selection and summarize them in a sentence

Suggested Texts

The Rainbow Fish

The Great Kapok Tree: A Tale of the Amazon Rain Forest

Summarizing seems easy for adults, but it's a challenge for many students. Figuring out which details make up the essence of the story can be tricky. Therefore, teachers often teach the "Someone/Wanted/So/But/Finally" framework to help students identify those important elements. When introducing the lesson, use the vertical graphic organizer on page 137; the blocks are large enough for all students to see when it's displayed for the class. To save paper, the form on page 138 can be duplicated to use with students. This variation provides room for two short books or two chapters in a long book. Students can record the example from your demonstration lesson in the first set of boxes and still have room for their own book.

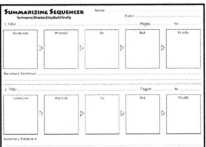

Step by Step:

1 Choose a short story or fairy tale with a clear sequence of events that follow the "Someone/Wanted/So/But/Finally" framework.

2 Display the chart, How to Write a Plot Summary (p. 135). Explain that it's easy to write a summary if you think about these five key elements. Explain the five parts and show the example from *The Three Little Pigs* on page 136.

3 Give students a blank Summarizing Sequencer graphic organizer (page 138) and read your selection aloud. Work together to complete the top set of frames and the summary sentence. If the summary is a long, run-on sentence, have them break it into two shorter sentences.

4 The next day, read another story and have students work with a partner or alone to follow the same steps and complete the bottom section.

HOW TO WRITE A PLOT SUMMARY

A good plot summary tells the most important events without including unnecessary details. To figure out which details are important, remember the key words *Someone/Wanted/So/But/Finally.* Ask yourself the questions below and use the answers to write a sentence or two that summarizes the story's plot.

SOMEONE — Who is the main character in this story or part of the story?

WANTED — What is the character's goal? What is he or she trying to accomplish?

SO — What did he or she do to try accomplish that goal?

BUT — What problem does the character face along the way?

FINALLY — What happened? How did the story end?

How to Write a Plot Summary
Someone/Wanted/So/But/Finally

Title: The Three Little Pigs   Pages: all   to: _____

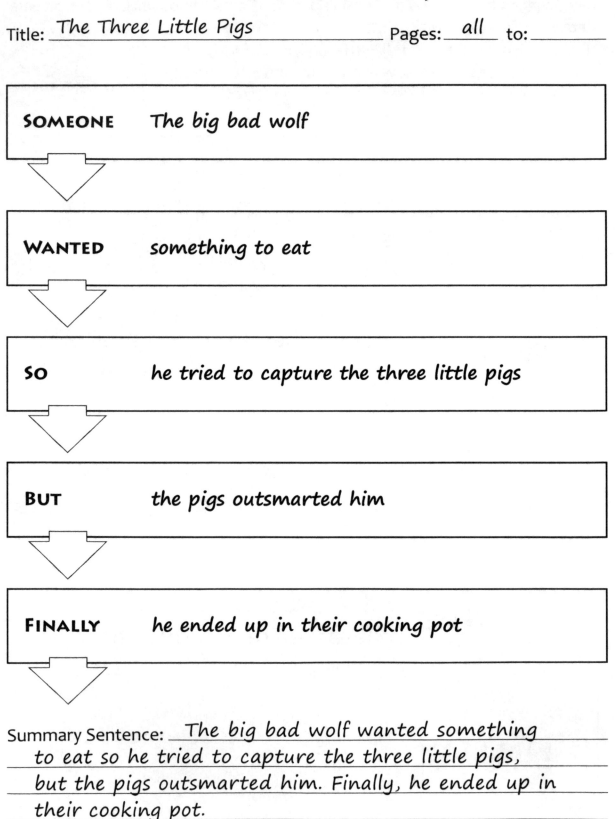

SOMEONE   The big bad wolf

WANTED   something to eat

SO   he tried to capture the three little pigs

BUT   the pigs outsmarted him

FINALLY   he ended up in their cooking pot

Summary Sentence: The big bad wolf wanted something to eat so he tried to capture the three little pigs, but the pigs outsmarted him. Finally, he ended up in their cooking pot.

How to Write a Plot Summary
Someone/Wanted/So/But/Finally

Title: _____ Pages: _____ to: _____

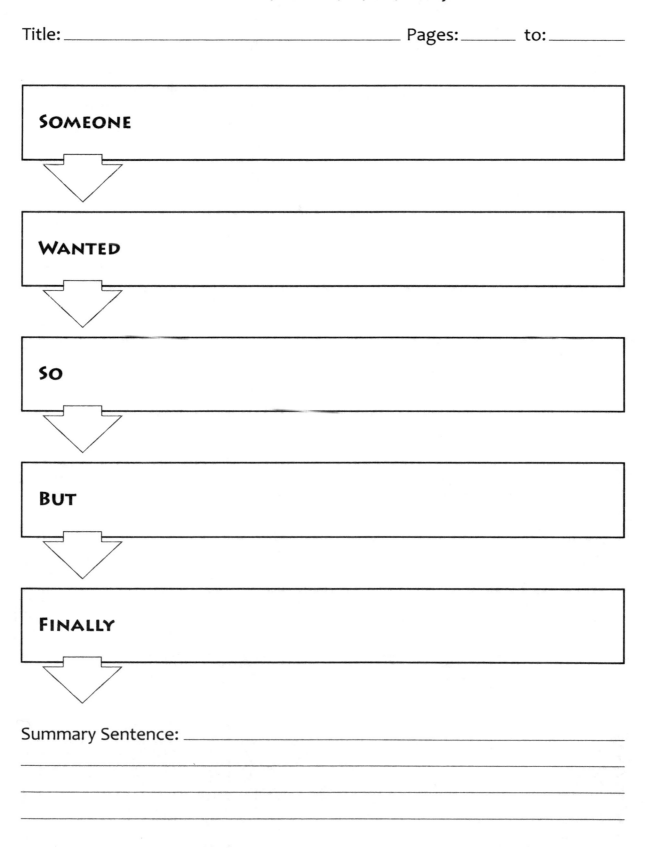

SOMEONE

WANTED

SO

BUT

FINALLY

Summary Sentence: _____
_____
_____
_____

Summarizing Sequencer

Someone/Wanted/So/But/Finally

Name: _____

Date: _____

1. Title: _____ Pages: _____ to _____

Someone	Wanted	So	But	Finally

Summary Sentence: _____

2. Title: _____ Pages: _____ to _____

Someone	Wanted	So	But	Finally

Summary Sentence: _____

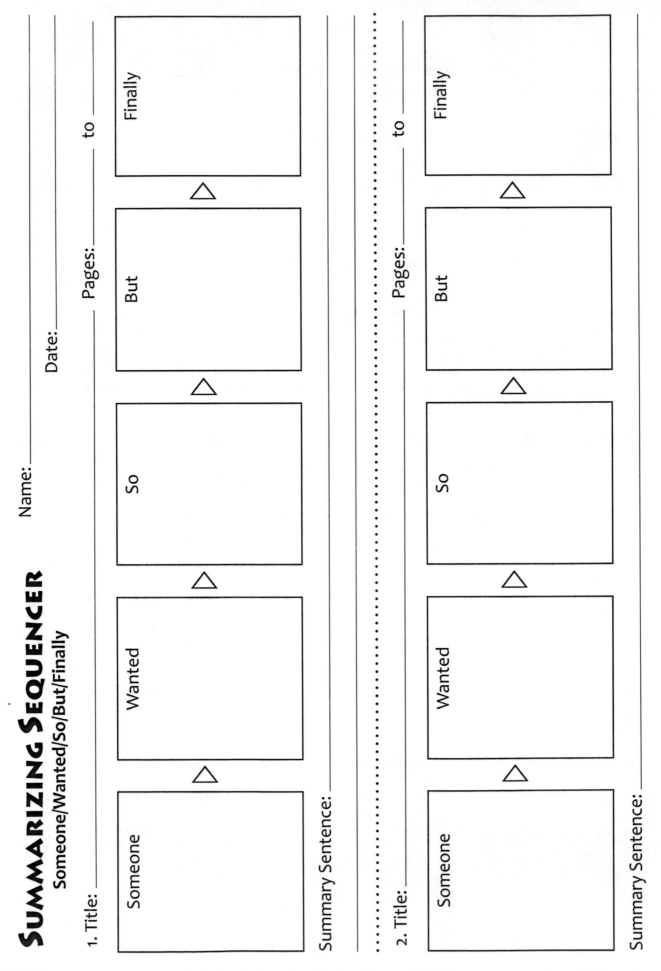

Story Map Variations

Reading Strategies

● Identify a story's characters, setting, and plot elements

Suggested Texts

Jack and the Beanstalk (Kellogg)

The Pumpkin Runner

Learning to identify the elements of a story is a component of most reading programs. Because different grade levels address this reading strategy in different ways, I include two variations of the Story Map. The first Story Map graphic organizer asks students to identify all story elements, including character, setting, and the basic plot sequence. The second Story Plot Map graphic organizer focuses only on the plot and takes students beyond the basic "beginning, middle, and end" generally taught in elementary school.

Step by Step:

1 Begin with the basic Story Map (p. 140). Read aloud a short story with a simple plot, and teach your students how to determine which events are found in the beginning, middle, and end. Explain that the beginning is where the author introduces the characters, and the reader then learns about what the character wants to do or accomplish. The middle is where the character often encounters a series of problems or obstacles. The conclusion or end is where the reader finds out what happens.

2 After students understand basic plot elements, read aloud another story with a more complex plot. Use the Story Plot Map on page 141 to introduce them to story "climax," the turning point of the action. The climax occurs between the middle and the conclusion, and it's the point just before the reader finds out how the story ends. The frames of the Story Plot Map are arranged to signify the rising and falling action of the story, and the illustrations provide additional clues about the types of events that occur in each part of the plot.

3 Both of these graphic organizers should be introduced in the usual way by teaching them in a whole-group lesson, then having students complete them with a partner, and finally, assigning them for independent practice.

STORY MAP

Name: _____

Date: _____

Title	Author
Setting	Characters

Beginning

Middle

End

Story Plot Map

Name: _____

Title: _____

Author: _____

Date: _____

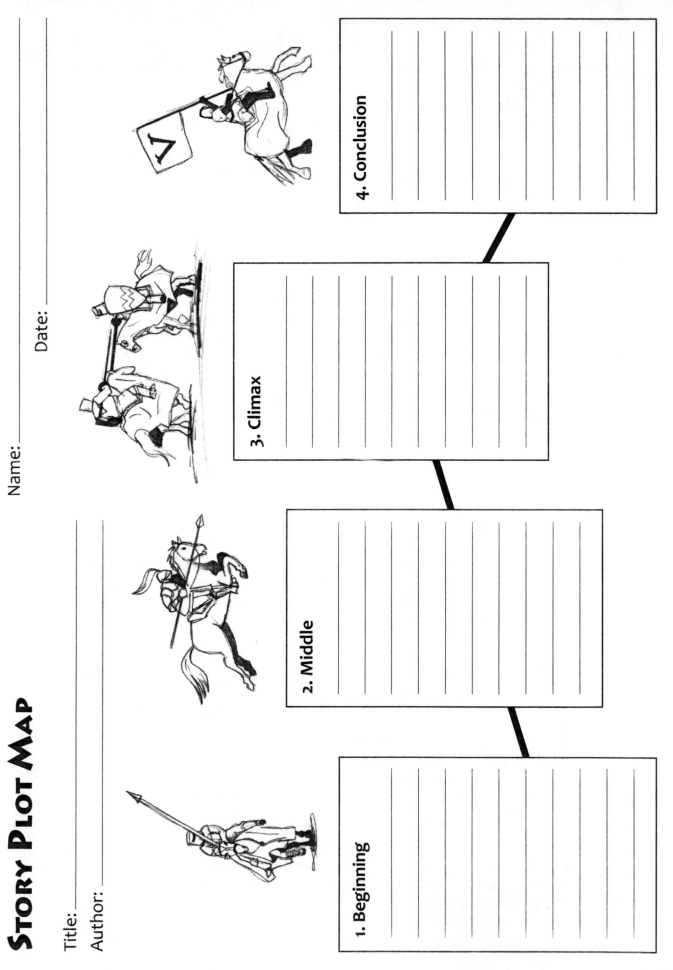

1. Beginning

2. Middle

3. Climax

4. Conclusion

Step-by-Step Predictions

Common Core Standards:
RL 4.1, RL 5.1, RL 6.1

Reading Strategies

- Making predictions based on details in a literature selection

- Revising predictions while reading to reflect new information

Suggested Texts

Two Bad Ants

Pink and Say

Good readers continually make predictions as they read. They usually don't stop to verbalize their predictions, but their thoughts are always reaching ahead to anticipate what's going to happen next. But many students think making predictions is an isolated event. They make one prediction and then read to find out if they're right or wrong. Step-by-Step Predictions guides them through the act of making a series of predictions as they constantly revise their initial predictions based on new evidence. This graphic organizer is a great one to use when reading any literature selection with an element of mystery or suspense.

Step by Step:

1 Select a short mystery story or play to read with your students. Give each student a blank copy of Step-by-Step Predictions (p. 143). Explain that good readers make predictions throughout the story based on the clues or hints that the author leaves about what's going to happen next. Ask them to read a page or two and have everyone stop at a given location.

2 Call on volunteers to share what they think is going to happen and record at least one detail or "clue" on which they based their predictions. Everyone completes the first part of the form with their own clues and predictions.

3 Read several more pages or an entire chapter, and have the students record more clues and another prediction based on this section. Explain that it's fine to change predictions based on new clues they have read. If they want to keep the same prediction, they should record additional clues that confirm their first prediction.

4 Ask students to read a little farther but not to the end of the story. Have them stop on a given page and make a third and final prediction, also recording the clues that led to that prediction. Have them finish the story and record what happened.

Name: _____ Date: _____

STEP-BY-STEP PREDICTIONS

From
Page #
_____

to
Page #
_____

Important Clues

1st Prediction

Important Clues

2nd Prediction

From
Page #
_____

to
Page #
_____

Important Clues

3rd Prediction

From
Page #
_____

to
Page #
_____

What Happened?

_____

Literary Response Scroll

Reading Strategies

● Recount stories, including fables and folktales from diverse cultures, and determine the central message, lesson, or moral

● Reflect on lesson or moral and write personal response

The Literary Response Scroll is a simple graphic organizer that can be used with any short story or folktale that has a theme, moral, or lesson. The form includes a place for students to summarize the events and identify at least one lesson or moral being conveyed by the story.

Suggested Texts

Fables

The Leprechaun's Gold

Step by Step:

1 Introduce the Literary Response Scroll by reading aloud a fable or folktale that has a fairly obvious moral or lesson.

2 Give each student a copy of the graphic organizer (p. 145) to complete as you work through it together. Ask them to help you summarize the folktale's events by referring to the Summarizing Sequencer graphic organizer (p. 134). Flesh out the resulting summary sentence with additional details to end up with a paragraph about what happened in the folktale.

3 Ask your students if they think there was a moral or lesson to the story. Have them discuss possible morals and lessons along with details about how those lessons are conveyed through the text. Write at least one moral or lesson in the middle of the graphic organizer.

4 Then ask your students how they feel personally about the folktale and its moral or message. Can they connect in any way with the message? Do they agree with the moral? If they had written the folktale, would they have written the ending the same way?

5 After they understand how to use this graphic organizer, have them read another folktale and complete it with a partner or on their own.

Name: _____ Date: _____

LITERARY RESPONSE SCROLL

Title: _____

Summary _____
_____
_____
_____
_____
_____
_____
_____
_____

Theme, Moral, or Lesson _____
_____
_____
_____

My Personal Response _____
_____
_____
_____
_____
_____
_____
_____

Poetry Peace Map

Reading Strategies

- Understand the literal and figurative meanings in poems

- Identify techniques used by the poet to convey meaning and emotion

Suggested Texts

A Writing Kind of Day: Poems for Young Poets

Knock at a Star: An Introduction to Children's Poetry

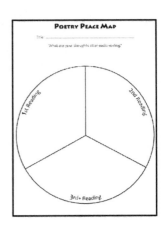

Many students struggle with poetry because they don't understand that even the shortest poems are often packed with meaning and symbolism. Whether poems are light-hearted or thought-provoking, the reader seldom unravels all of the shades of meaning with one reading. The Poetry Peace Map helps students extract more meaning from poetry.

Step by Step:

1 Display a poem that has many layers of meaning.

2 Give each student a copy of the Poetry Peace Map (p. 148) and then talk them through the directions on page 147. Ask everyone to read the poem just one time and write what they think it means in the first section. If they have no idea, it's okay to write **no idea**.

3 Have them read the poem again more carefully and complete the second section.

4 Ask them to read it as many times as needed to grasp not only the meaning, but to locate and record poetic techniques used such as imagery, personification, or alliteration. Discuss and share these findings as a class.

LAURA'S Tips

Students can sketch a peace symbol in their reading journals instead of duplicating the graphic organizer.

POETRY PEACE MAP

What are your thoughts after each reading?

1st Reading - Read the poem one time slowly and carefully. What do you think the poem is about? Record your thoughts.

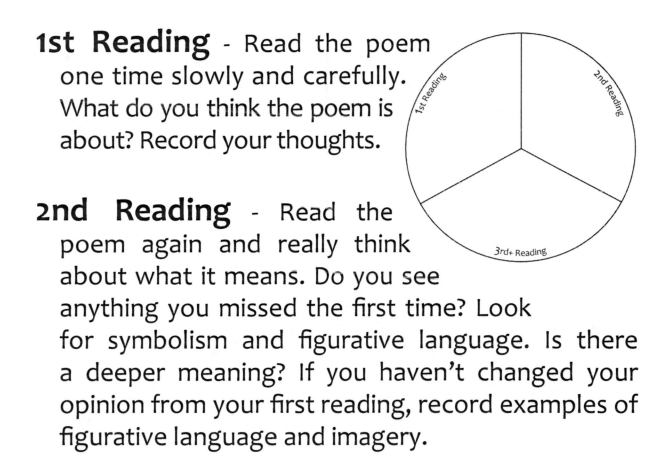

2nd Reading - Read the poem again and really think about what it means. Do you see anything you missed the first time? Look for symbolism and figurative language. Is there a deeper meaning? If you haven't changed your opinion from your first reading, record examples of figurative language and imagery.

3rd+ Reading - Read it again, as many times as needed to understand the poem fully. Record any additional thoughts or feelings about the poem. What techniques did the poet use to convey his or her message?

Name: _____ Date: _____

Poetry Peace Map

Title: _____

What are your thoughts after each reading?

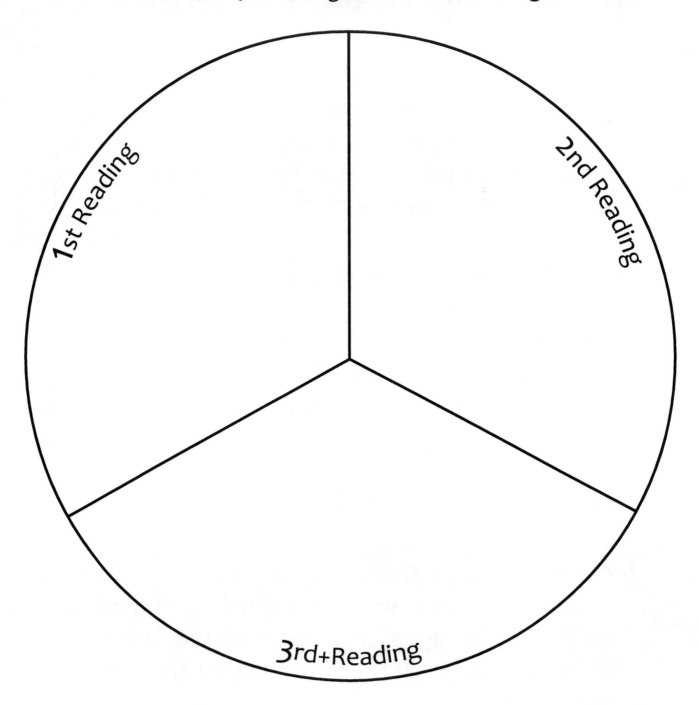

1st Reading

2nd Reading

3rd+Reading

Poetic Reflections

Common Core Standards:
RL 2.10, RL 3.5, RL 3.10, RL 4.2,
RL 4.10, RL 5.2, RL 5.10, RL 6.10

Reading Strategies

- Understand the literal and figurative meanings in poems
- Identify techniques used by the poet to convey meaning and emotion
- Examine and record personal responses

Suggested Texts

Owl Moon

Poetry for Young People: Maya Angelou

The Poetic Reflections graphic organizer offers a way for students to go beyond basic poetry analysis to share their own personal responses. This graphic organizer works best after introducing the Poetry Peace Map (p. 146) because students need to understand how to read a poem multiple times, looking for deeper meaning. Because they are asked for a personal response, students should be allowed to choose their own poems for this activity.

Step by Step:

1 Before the lesson, check out a selection of poetry books from your media center for students to use when selecting their poems. Introduce Poetic Reflections by modeling the graphic organizer (p. 150) with one of your favorite poems. Show them how to record what the poem is about in the top bubble.

2 Analyze the techniques the poet uses to convey that meaning and write those details in the second bubble.

3 Describe your own personal response, including feelings and connections, and model how to record those details. Ask questions to prompt the students: Are they able to make any connections? Does the poem make them wonder about something or feel a particular emotion?

4 Have the students use the Poetic Reflections graphic organizer with a poem each has selected individually.

POETIC REFLECTIONS

Name: _____ Date: _____

Poem: _____ Poet: _____

What is the poem about?
_____
_____
_____
_____
_____
_____

What poetic techniques are used?
_____
_____
_____
_____
_____
_____
_____

What is your personal response?
_____
_____
_____
_____
_____
_____

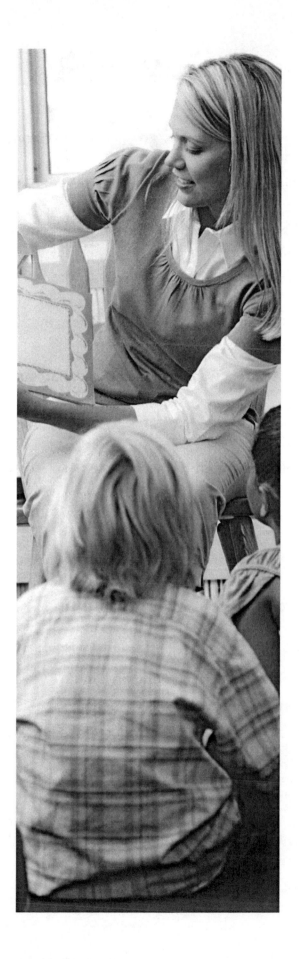

• • • • • • • • •

Bibliography of
Suggested Texts

BIBLIOGRAPHY OF SUGGESTED TEXTS

Adams, Simon. *The Best Book of Volcanoes*. New York: Kingfisher, 2007.

Angelou, Maya. *Poetry for Young People: Maya Angelou*. Edited by Edwin Graves Wilson. Illustrated by Jerome Lagarrigue. New York: Sterling, 2007.

Arnold, Marsha Diane. *The Pumpkin Runner*. Illustrated by Brad Sneed. New York: Dial Books for Young Readers, 1998.

Blume, Judy. *The Pain and the Great One*. Illustrated by Irene Trivas. Scarsdale: Bradbury Press, 1984.

Brown, Margaret Wise. *The Important Book*. Illustrated by Leonard Weisgard. New York: HarperCollins, 1949.

Bunting, Eve. *Train to Somewhere*. Illustrated by Ronald Himler. New York: Clarion, 1996.

Cannon, Janell. *Crickwing*. San Diego: Harcourt, 2000.

Cherry, Lynne. *The Great Kapok Tree: A Tale of the Amazon Rain Forest*. San Diego: Harcourt Brace & Company, 1990.

Cole, Joanna. *The Magic School Bus and the Electric Field Trip*. Illustrated by Bruce Degen. New York: Scholastic, 1997.

Edwards, Pamela Duncan. *The Leprechaun's Gold*. Illustrated by Henry Cole. New York: Katherine Tegen Books, 2004.

Fletcher, Ralph J. *A Writing Kind of Day: Poems for Young Poets*. Illustrated by April Ward. Honesdale, PA: Boyds Mills Press, 2005.

Gibbons, Gail. *Nature's Green Umbrella: Tropical Rain Forests*. New York: Mulberry Books, 1997.

Hopkinson, Deborah. *Sweet Clara and the Freedom Quilt*. Illustrated by James Ransome. New York: Knopf, 1993.

Lobel, Arnold. *Fables*. New York: Harper Collins, 1980.

Kalman, Bobbie. *The Wagon Train*. New York: Crabtree Publishing Company, 1998.

Kellogg, Steven. *Jack and the Beanstalk*. New York: William Morrow & Company, 1991.

Kennedy, X. J., and Dorothy M. Kennedy. *Knock at a Star: A Child's Introduction to Poetry*. Illustrated by Karen Ann Weinhaus. Boston: Little, Brown, 1982.

Krull, Kathleen. *Wilma Unlimited: How Wilma Rudolph Became the World's Fastest Woman*. Illustrated by David Diaz. San Diego: Harcourt Brace, 1996.

Lessem, Don. *National Geographic Kids Ultimate Dinopedia: The Most Complete Dinosaur Reference Ever*. Illustrated by Franco Tempesta. Washington, DC: National Geographic Children's Books, 2010.

Locker, Thomas. *Water Dance*. San Diego: Harcourt Children's Books, 1997.

Lynette, Rachel. *Gravity: Forces and Motion.* Chicago: Heinemann-Raintree, 2008.

Mack, Lorrie. *Eyewonder: Weather.* New York: DK Children, 2004.

Martin, Rafe. *The Rough-face Girl.* Illustrated by David Shannon. New York: G.P. Putnam's Sons, 1992.

Munson, Derek. *Enemy Pie.* Illustrated by Tara Calahan King. San Francisco: Chronicle Books, 2000.

Osborne, Will, and Mary Pope Osborne. *Magic Tree House Fact Tracker #1: Titanic: A Nonfiction Companion to "Tonight on the Titanic."* Illustrated by Sal Murdocca. New York: Random House, 2002.

Pascal, Janet. *Who Was Dr. Seuss?* Illustrated by Nancy Harrison. New York, NY: Grosset & Dunlap, 2011.

Patrick, Denise Lewis. *Jackie Robinson: Strong Inside and Out.* New York: HarperCollins, 2005.

Pfister, Marcus. *The Rainbow Fish.* New York: North-South Books, 1992.

Polacco, Patricia. *Pink and Say.* New York: Philomel Books, 1994.

Rappaport, Doreen. *Martin's Big Words: The Life of Dr. Martin Luther King, Jr.* Illustrated by Bryan Collier. New York: Hyperion Books for Children, 2001.

Schotter, Roni, and Kyrsten Brooker. *Nothing Ever Happens on 90th Street.* New York: Orchard Books, 1997.

Shannon, David. *A Bad Case of Stripes.* New York: Blue Sky Press, 1998.

Steig, William. *Sylvester and the Magic Pebble.* New York: Windmill Books, 1969.

Thaler, Mike, and Jared D. Lee. *The Teacher from the Black Lagoon.* New York: Scholastic, 2008.

Van Allsburg, Chris. *The Wretched Stone.* Boston: Houghton Mifflin, 1991.

Van Allsburg, Chris. *Two Bad Ants.* Boston: Houghton Mifflin, 1988.

Yolen, Jane, and Heidi E. Y. Stemple. *The Mary Celeste: An Unsolved Mystery from History.* Illustrated by Roger Roth. New York: Simon & Schuster Books for Young Readers, 1999.

Yolen, Jane. *Owl Moon.* Illustrated by John Schoenherr. New York: Philomel Books, 1987.

NOTES

NOTES

NOTES

NOTES

NOTES

About the Author

Laura Candler is a teacher with 30 years of classroom experience in grades 4 through 6. She has a Master's Degree in Elementary Education, National Board Certification as a Middle Childhood Generalist, and was a Milken Family Foundation Award winner in 2000.

Laura is the author of books and materials that help teachers implement new teaching strategies. Her work bridges the gap between educational theory and practice. Through her materials and her dynamic, interactive workshops, she gives teachers the tools they need to implement teaching strategies immediately.

Laura's materials are "field tested, teacher approved." They have been used by thousands of real teachers in real classrooms all over the world. Laura modifies and adapts her programs based on the experience of those teachers.

For more information and resources, go to Laura Candler's Teaching Resources website at www.lauracandler.com.

About Compass and Brigantine Media

Compass is the educational books imprint of publisher Brigantine Media. Materials created by real education practitioners are the hallmark of Compass books. For more information, please contact:

Neil Raphel
Brigantine Media | 211 North Avenue | Saint Johnsbury, Vermont | 05819
Phone: 802-751-8802
E-mail: neil@brigantinemedia.com | Website: www.brigantinemedia.com

Also by Laura Candler:
Laura Candler's Power Reading Workshop: A Step-by-Step Guide

Laura Candler's
POWER READING WORKSHOP
A STEP-BY-STEP GUIDE

Reading opens up the world for your students.

Laura Candler's Power Reading Workshop: A Step-by-Step Guide will help you teach your students to love reading. Designed by award-winning teacher Laura Candler, this book walks you through the first ten days to implement a basic Reading Workshop with your students. Then Laura shows you how to add twelve proven "Power Reading Tools" to the program to make your Reading Workshop the most effective reading instruction you will ever use. Students and teachers alike love the simplicity, fun, and excitement of Laura's Power Reading Workshop program.

Everything you need, including reproducible worksheets, charts, and forms, are included to help you implement a Power Reading Workshop in your classroom today. Teachers around the world have used Laura's straightforward approach with fantastic results—that's what makes her program "field tested and teacher approved."

For more information, go to:
www.powerreadingworkshop.com

● ● ● ● ●

COMPASS
A DIVISION OF BRIGANTINE MEDIA

CPSIA information can be obtained at www.ICGtesting.com
Printed in the USA
LVOW09s2200010916

502890LV00010B/44/P